Future Metaphysics

Theory Redux series

Series editor: Laurent de Sutter

Published Titles

Alfie Bown, *The Playstation Dreamworld*

Laurent de Sutter, *Narcocapitalism*

Roberto Esposito, *Persons and Things*

Graham Harman, *Immaterialism*

Srećko Horvat, *The Radicality of Love*

Dominic Pettman, *Infinite Distraction*

Nick Srnicek, *Platform Capitalism*

Helen Hester, *Xenofeminism*

Franco Berardi, *The Second Coming*

Armen Avanessian, *Future Metaphysics*

Future Metaphysics

Armen Avanessian

Translated by James C. Wagner

polity

Copyright © Armen Avanessian 2020

This English edition © Polity Press, 2020

Polity Press
65 Bridge Street
Cambridge CB2 1UR, UK

Polity Press
101 Station Landing
Suite 300
Medford, MA 02155, USA

ISBN-13: 978-1-5095-3796-9 (hardback)
ISBN-13: 978-1-5095-3797-6 (paperback)

A catalogue record for this book is available from the British Library.

Library of Congress Cataloging-in-Publication Data
Names: Avanessian, Armen, author. | Wagner, James A., translator.
Title: Future metaphysics / Armen Avanessian ; translated by James C. Wagner
Other titles: Metaphysik zur Zeit. English
Description: Medford : Polity, 2020. | Series: Theory redux series | Translated from German. | Includes bibliographical references and index. | Summary: "This book is an attempt at restating the importance of the great metaphysical categories of substance and accident, form and matter, life and death for the present: how our contemporary predicament forces us both to reclaim them and to give them a radically new twist"-- Provided by publisher.
Identifiers: LCCN 2019023993 (print) | LCCN 2019023994 (ebook) | ISBN 9781509537969 (hardback) | ISBN 9781509537976 (paperback) | ISBN 9781509537983 (epub)
Subjects: LCSH: Metaphysics.
Classification: LCC BD113 .A9313 2020 (print) | LCC BD113 (ebook) | DDC 110--dc23
LC record available at https://lccn.loc.gov/2019023993
LC ebook record available at https://lccn.loc.gov/2019023994

Typeset in 12.5/15 Adobe Garamond by
Servis Filmsetting Ltd, Stockport, Cheshire
Printed and bound in Great Britain by CPI Group (UK) Ltd, Croydon

The publisher has used its best endeavours to ensure that the URLs for external websites referred to in this book are correct and active at the time of going to press. However, the publisher has no responsibility for the websites and can make no guarantee that a site will remain live or that the content is or will remain appropriate.

Every effort has been made to trace all copyright holders, but if any have been overlooked the publisher will be pleased to include any necessary credits in any subsequent reprint or edition.

For further information on Polity, visit our website: politybooks.com

Contents

Acknowledgments

This book began with a spontaneous request in early 2018 from Francesco Manacorda, Artistic Director of the V-A-C Foundation. I was invited to curate a large-scale exhibition at the Moscow Museum of Modern Art (MMOMA) that summer, which would involve me writing roughly ten short texts – on the topic of my choice – for as many rooms of the museum. The thematic freedom, along with the experimental opportunity to frame the rooms of the exhibition – itself a rehearsal for a future institution currently under construction – as the chapters of a yet-to-be-written book, allowed me to compose, undisturbed, what ultimately grew to far more than just ten wall or catalog entries, all of which found their way into this equally spontaneous book.

Of course, many of the ideas and motifs collected here have occupied me for quite some time, not least in collaborative works with close colleagues such as Victoria Ivanova (on the question of institutional realism) and especially Anke Hennig, with whom I was working on a book about questions of technology, politics, and gender at the same time as I was writing this one. I would like once again to express my gratitude to Bernd Klöckner and Joseph Wallace Goodhew for their editorial supervision of the German original. Many thanks as well to everyone at Polity Press who worked together with me on this project, including Elise Heslinga, John Thompson, my translator James C. Wagner, and especially Laurent de Sutter for inviting me to publish this book as part of his series.

This book was written, with a strong feeling of expectation, for the future (and initially dedicated to my "future family"). That future has since arrived as a joyous present. I dedicate this book to my son Adrian.

Introduction: Metaphysics

Origin of man now proved. – Metaphysics must flourish. –
He who understands baboon would do more towards metaphysics than Locke.

Charles Darwin

BAD TIMES, BUT GOOD TIMES FOR METAPHYSICS
– Our society is suffering at every level from overwhelming challenges and crises of meaning that we have forgotten to conceive as metaphysical. The leaps in technology or advances in physics and other natural sciences that once sallied forth to alleviate or even liberate us entirely from our earthly problems are not necessarily of any further help to us. To the contrary, we are increasingly

confronted by collateral damage from modernity's technological revolutions (climate change, for example) that threatens the life forms of our planet – humanity included – and thus more than ever raises questions which cannot be approached empirically.

Even where the triumphs of modern science have indisputably led to improvements in the quality of life and longer lives overall, ever increasing life expectancies and the transhumanist fantasy of unending life give rise to new metaphysical questions on a par with those concerning the possible disappearance of our species. To put it dramatically, whether eternal life is imminent or the human race as a whole is at risk of going extinct in what has pointedly been dubbed the "Anthropocene" age – a world dominated by transhuman *"Homo" sapiens* and a world without humans both confront us to an unprecedented degree with metaphysical problems.

RETIRING THE *ANIMAL LABORANS* – Human beings are natural-born philosophers. To be human, Martin Heidegger once wrote to his mistress Elisabeth Blochmann, is to philosophize, and the philosophical tradition is filled with definitions of man as an *animal metaphysicum* and *animal rationale*. This metaphysical and rational animal is also a working animal, an *animal laborans*. And indeed, philosophers, no less than sociologists and economists (revolutionary as well as bourgeois), have traditionally agreed that man may be defined through his labor as *Homo faber*.

With the establishment of modern capitalism beginning in the sixteenth century, and industrialization in the eighteenth century, the lives of most working- and middle-class people (at first primarily men) came to be defined, and their conceptions of themselves shaped, by their occupation and employment. Today, however, the notion that an occupation lends human life *internal stability* (Helmut Schelsky) is at best only partly true. It is rather much more a major source of bourgeois insecurity, not least because the boundaries between work and non-work have become fluid. According to the sociologist and renowned expert on risk Ulrich Beck, the system of standardized full employment – familiar only since the latter half of the twentieth century, and often assumed to be the normal condition of liberal capitalist societies – "is beginning to soften and fray at the margins into flexibilizations of its three supporting pillars: labor law, work site, and working hours."[1] The *animal laborans* is thus becoming problematic in an entirely new way, regardless of whether we are talking about physical or intellectual labor (if such a distinction – itself metaphysical – were still at all appropriate).

ON HEAVEN AND EARTH – Disparaging or pitying remarks about philosophers being out of touch with the world are as old as philosophy itself, dating back at least to the sixth century BCE, when a Thracian maiden famously mocked Thales of Miletus for falling into a well while gazing up at the sky. A well-worn prejudice has it that metaphysics stands in direct contradiction to reality, making it a hopelessly obsolete or old-fashioned way of thinking. Metaphysical thought's dubious reputation can also be seen in the negative connotations that the word "speculation" has taken on over time. Particularly since the advent of modernity two centuries ago, it has often been employed as a purely pejorative term: "mere speculation" in the sense of baseless ratiocination untethered from reality.

Books on the history of modern philosophy report a turn away from naive belief in philosophy's ability to come to grips with matters directly and toward an epistemology that precedes all established knowledge. Philosophy's metaphysical or speculative energies have never truly abated, however, not least because metaphysical questions always have historical connotations and thus continually reemerge as we grapple with currently prevailing sciences and technologies. Perhaps philosophy's speculative energies always experience an upsurge anytime there is a technological revolution. The first Ionian and Greek cosmologies and natural philosophies elaborated by Anaximenes, Anaximander, and Thales would then also be responses to the acquisition of writing, the settling down of *Homo sapiens*, and the accompanying transition to agriculture.

Thales, for example, according to a less widely circulated anecdote, is supposed to have come into his wealth as a direct result of his knowledge of astronomy, which allowed him to predict the yield of olive harvests. The rise of modern philosophy likewise cannot be separated from the invention of the printing press, nor the emergence of new speculative approaches today, from the need to respond to digitalization, which – as is becoming ever clearer, although it only began a few decades ago – is radically transforming our society.

MANDATORY MEMBERSHIP IN A CLUB NO ONE WANTS TO BELONG TO – If we look at the modern history of metaphysics, particularly that of the last few centuries, we notice a tendency among philosophers to toil away at what they believe to be unresolved metaphysical questions in the work of their predecessors. The "crusher of everything" Immanuel Kant did this with the skeptic David Hume; the pessimist Arthur Schopenhauer with Kant; the self-proclaimed "transvaluer of all values" Friedrich Nietzsche with Schopenhauer; Martin Heidegger with Nietzsche's frantic efforts to turn the history of metaphysics upside down by taking recourse back to pre-Socratic philosophies; Jacques Derrida with Heidegger, with the insight that metaphysics ultimately cannot be overcome ...

At the same time, of course, we can also observe historical shifts that shed light on the changes in meaning of what various epochs have understood as metaphysics. In the early modern period, with the renaissance of philosophy in the sixteenth century, we see increasingly sharp critiques from humanists such as Rabelais, Montaigne, and Erasmus against university philosophers, whom they considered to be irrelevant and out of touch with or even hostile to life (since which time words like "academic," "scholastic," and "metaphysics" have often had a negative ring to them).

In parallel with this, the orientation of those philosophers who dedicated themselves to metaphysics also changed in terms of content. Indeed, the rationalists of the seventeenth and eighteenth centuries (e.g. Descartes, Spinoza, and Leibniz) covered a far greater range of topics than did, say, the theologians of the Middle Ages. Metaphysicians now occupied themselves not only with eternal being, the highest substance, or God, but also with a host of related questions: man's relation to God, the essence of the mortal or immortal soul, the connection between body and mind, the problem of the possibility or impossibility of free will in sensual beings, etc. Put bluntly, all those questions that could not easily be assigned to another philosophical discipline such as logic, epistemology, or ethics were henceforth deemed to be metaphysical. It is no coincidence that this same period gave birth to "ontology," that discipline which deals with questions of being, existence, or substance, what for centuries prior had been considered the true object of metaphysics.

WHAT WE TALK ABOUT WHEN WE'RE NOT SURE WHAT WE'RE TALKING ABOUT – The self-critical reorientation and reinvention of metaphysics in modernity also correlates with an *essential* change – in the full meaning of that word – in what metaphysics previously had dealt with, namely, an immutable, everlasting, substantial, divine essence or the true being or nature of all that which exists. As physics and other increasingly "empirical" and natural sciences dedicated themselves to this nature, submitting *physis* to their categorizing grip, the branch of philosophical thought called meta-physics naturally had to reorient itself. Owing to its high degree of abstraction, not even the rationalistic realignment of philosophy ushered in by Descartes was immune to renewed criticism by empiricist thinkers such as Hobbes, Hume, and Berkeley. These critiques were joined in the eighteenth century by skeptical positions that posited the impossibility of metaphysics or even went so far as to deny that it had any right or reason to exist. Its questions were somewhere between unanswerable (according to milder skeptics) and meaningless (according to more radical critics); in any case, there was no point in getting oneself mixed up in metaphysical adventures or the adventure of metaphysics.

A fundamental difficulty in defining metaphysics certainly lies in the fact that there is no prevailing consensus as to its object. Does it even have an object, in the way that biology explores life or economics the field of the economy? Aristotle's definition of the object of metaphysics as the highest of all things had long-lasting repercussions (extending well beyond medieval philosophy). Unlike other philosophical disciplines, such as ethics or logic, he asserted, metaphysics was concerned with the divine, the prime mover (itself unmoved), or, in less theological terms, with (immutable) being as such, the substance underlying everything, or with purely logical principles such as the law of identity (A=A).

If conversely, however, as Alexander Gottlieb Baumgarten postulated in the mid eighteenth century, *metaphysica est scientia prima cognitionis humanae principia continens*: i.e. if metaphysics is that science which contains the first principles of human knowledge, then does it still have a timeless object at all, beyond things that can be known? Or does it now only occupy itself narcissistically with human knowledge itself? Like Buster Keaton at the end of Samuel Beckett's *Film*, finally free of all pursuers and outside interests, philosophy, late in its career, looks itself in the eye and is startled to find that there is hardly anything left to see when one sees only oneself. Philo-sophy is constantly in danger of losing sight of what it ought to know due to its sheer occupation with or love of knowing.

A SCIENCE WITHOUT AN OBJECT? – "Metaphysics is a questioning in which we inquire into beings as a whole, and inquire in such a way that in so doing we ourselves, the questioners, are thereby also included in the question, placed into question. Accordingly, fundamental concepts are not universals, not some formulae for the universal properties of a field of objects (such as animals or language). Rather they are concepts of a properly peculiar kind. In each case, they comprehend the whole within themselves, they are *comprehensive concepts*. [...] Metaphysical thinking is comprehensive thinking in this double sense. It deals with the whole and it grips existence through and through."[2] With such pronouncements, Martin Heidegger sought to uncover once again the radicality of philosophical questioning, its ability to get to the root of things. Elsewhere, he writes: "[I]t is not just that the object of philosophy does not lie at hand, but philosophy has no object at all. Philosophy is a happening that must at all times work out Being for itself anew [...]. Only in this happening does philosophical truth open up."[3] The question then is whether philosophy's lack of an object represents the final blow to its already dubious reputation or whether, on the contrary, it offers it an advantage. For in the modern era – that is, after *God is dead* (Nietzsche) and the notion of an eternal substance can no longer be presupposed as self-evident – the fact that metaphysics must always first prove that it has a reason and right to exist can also be seen as an opportunity. Perhaps its potential lies precisely in its peculiar objectlessness. For "beyond the object" in no way means the same thing as "beyond all objectivity" or "purely subjective."

NO BEGINNING OR END IN SIGHT – If we take a look back to the fourth century BCE at the supposed inventor of the discipline, it becomes apparent that Aristotle himself did not actually write any "Metaphysics." Indeed, the word does not even appear in any of his writings. (He writes instead of "first philosophy" or "first science.") The assumption that his *Metaphysics* is concerned with something *behind* or *above* the realm of the physical is as widespread as it is mistaken. Rather, the work that founded an entire tradition owes its title to an editorial problem.

Around a hundred years after Aristotle's death, a certain Andronicus of Rhodes found himself faced with the question of what title the four-teen books or book chapters following Aristotle's *Physics* should be collected under. The order-loving editor decided on *Ta meta ta physika* or, roughly translated, "the [writings] after the *Physics*" ("*meta*" here referring to a spatial arrangement, i.e. meaning "*behind*"). It may be that in choosing such a pragmatic title, the philologist wanted to keep younger students – philosophical thought having first been institutionalized in an academic context beginning with Aristotle's teacher Plato – from reading these texts prematurely. The fact that the topics and reflections in Aristotle's books on physics are also thoroughly "metaphysical" speaks against this hypothesis, however.

Long story short, whenever we set foot in the field of metaphysics, we find ourselves faced with a similar problem: we cannot find a beginning anywhere. And is it any wonder that something without a proper beginning also comes to no end?

PHYSIS AFTER *META* – Regardless of whether we understand it spatially or logically, the name "metaphysics" always implies a relation to *physis* or, incautiously translated, to nature (the Latin translation of the Greek *physis* being *natura*, related to *natus*, "what is born"). And in fact, the history of metaphysics could be told with recourse to different concepts of nature.

Our understanding of metaphysics has always changed in line with debates about what was considered to be "nature" or "natural" at a given time. Put bluntly, and with a view to the problematic discipline itself: In the past, the legitimacy of metaphysics was always argued over with respect to what contemporaries understood to be the legitimate science of nature or what at a certain point in modernity came to be called the "natural sciences." For the fact that our first engagement with *physis* or *natura* was metaphysical has long since ceased to serve as a justification for conducting metaphysical philosophy of nature – gratitude is, gratefully, not a scientific category.

PHILOSOPHY OR SCIENCE – The history of philosophy could be described as that of a centuries-long evasive maneuver in reaction to scientific advances. What began with the Greeks as the natural-philosophical unity of observing concrete nature and meta-physically speculating beyond it seems to be able to participate in its own successes only in a limited way. The achievements of metaphysical engagement with nature gave rise to to the independent science of physics, and the problematization of life – to take a more recent example from the late eighteenth century – to the new discipline of biology. This evidently led not to greater confidence in the probative force of speculative questioning, but rather to philosophy once again being driven out of a region that it itself had once surveyed. Owing not least to the hegemony of mathematical rationality, any form of thought that does not present itself as a scientific explanation of the world is consistently dismissed as naively preliminary or methodologically deficient.

But are ultimate explanations even the point?

And what sort of scientific or rather science-generating concepts of advancement are we talking about? Advances in explanations, in new problems, or in discovered topics? Advances in answers and solutions, or in techniques and methods for asking the right questions in the first place? It might even be the case that, as the legal historian Eugen Rosenstock-Huessy once put it, scientific *solutions* are already there *before the problems* they are meant to solve, only we are not yet advanced enough to apply them.

SCIENCE AND PHILOSOPHY – One popular account has it that Western philosophy first blossomed with the coming together of Ionian natural philosophies and the mathematically based theories of Parmenides of Elea (in what is now southern Italy). In Athens, Socrates, and especially Plato, then began a long involvement with science (and particularly mathematics) that philosophy has never since relinquished. Philosophy and science have always been in close communication with and problematized each other.

Not without reason, many philosophers, as different as Karl Popper and Alain Badiou, have recalled the need for philosophy to be mathematically oriented. It is not enough simply to reflect *back* philosophically on scientific revolutions, whether the theory of relativity, quantum physics, or genetic engineering. Popper's deliberations rather suggest that behind every scientific or technological paradigm there is a metaphysical research program, "a set of non-testable propositions that are assumed to be true without any attempt having been made to challenge them."[4] Or, in the words of Catherine Malabou: "Be it in the form of a union, a cooperation, a hierarchization, a clarification or a divorce, philosophy cannot sustain itself without determining its own situation *vis-à-vis* science, and this has nothing to do with a mimicking. This is reciprocal, as sciences, be they 'hard' or 'human,' cannot but proceed from principles that contain concepts that have to be philosophically interrogated to the extent that they are not entirely objective, empirical, or positive."[5]

THESIS AND ANTITHESIS WITHOUT SYNTHESIS: THE SPECULATIVE PRAXIS OF THE NATURAL SCIENCES – What if the natural sciences have not simply replaced (natural) philosophy, but nor can the two peacefully coexist in a shared epistemic space?

What if modern science in particular itself has a speculative dimension, one that has only become evident over the past two centuries during which philosophy has so emphatically sought to rid itself of its own metaphysical dimension? It may well be that – paradoxically enough – the speculative dimension of the natural sciences evolved in parallel with philosophy's own frantic attempts to "despeculate" itself. The pessimistic philosopher of speed and dromological nihilist Paul Virilio may have offered the most radical articulation of this with his claim that what science and technology actually develop is the unknown and non-rational.

This in no way means that the natural sciences themselves are under suspicion of being secretly irrational, as though this would give free rein to always metaphysical philosophy. The point is rather to call attention to the whirl of formerly unknown open questions that emerge with every new science, and to note that speculative theorizing and speculative praxis are also characteristic precisely of the natural sciences. With no judgment implied, the natural sciences are on the move in speculative domains. Mathematics, too (as we should bear in mind particularly in the age of the algorithm), is anything but empirical; rather it is highly speculative, and not only since the invention of differential calculus and imaginary numbers.

Even more so with respect to scientific praxis, a speculative dimension of the production of scientific knowledge cannot be denied. Testing certain hypotheses often requires the use of complex devices (which not infrequently lead to entirely different and in this sense unintended insights and discoveries). Even following the implementation of atomic physics, its insights remain utterly meta-physical. In contrast to our devices and machines, whose calculations and results we then translate in terms of our own world of experience, no human being has ever had any empirical experience of individual atoms or molecules. The same holds true for the objects of sciences as different as cosmology and paleontology. Records emerge and the (assumption of the) existence of things like electrons or chemical elements becomes stabilized only indirectly or speculatively, e.g. through the repeated occurrence of a particular state or condition in a certain device, and in conjunction with corresponding social practices on the part of scientists. And is not the fantastic periodic table of chemical elements not one of the greatest – and until further notice incomplete, i.e. not entirely filled in – speculative designs or constructs there is, a concept of systematization with which science once again masks its speculative dimension? At any rate, it is not the case, as Heidegger thought, that science does not think. Rather, it does so in such a speculative way that it prefers to conceal this fact from itself and the world.

THE METAPHYSICAL SPECTERS OF SCIENCE – The philosopher of science Bruno Latour points to the numerous impurities and conflicts within individual (although strictly speaking always hybrid) sciences in various of his works. The long-lasting disputes surrounding the development of microbiology (Pasteur's hypothesis that life could be called forth or made to disappear as a result of changes in temperature initially sounded like utter nonsense); the theory of "genes," deeply metaphysical before its scientific ennoblement; the introduction of quasi-geophysiological actors in geological debates about the Anthropocene today – these are all examples of the understandable resistance of established knowledge that can see behind new actors only the specters of the past at work.

On their face, microbes, genes, and an active atmosphere are in fact ghostly reminders of the forgotten metaphysical origins of methodologically strict contemplation of nature. But what if scientific progress is only possible by grappling with science's speculative context? It may well be, as Latour explains, that "science proceeds not through the simple *expansion* of an already existing 'scientific worldview' but through the *revision* of the list of objects that populate the world, something that philosophers normally and rightly call a *metaphysics* and that the anthropologists call a *cosmology*." Hence "the word 'metaphysics' should not be so shocking for active scientists [...]. Metaphysics is the reserve, always to be refurbished, of physics."[6]

WHEN NATURE NO LONGER HEEDS ITS OWN LAWS – "It is an hypothesis that the sun will rise tomorrow: and this means that we do not *know* whether it will rise."[7] This sentence toward the end of Ludwig Wittgenstein's *Tractatus Logico-Philosophicus* is remarkable in multiple respects. In order to get a sense of just how wild a statement it is, one must set it apart from a long tradition of skeptical philosophies or worldviews, as though it were only saying that we cannot see into the future and thus cannot say whether the sun will not actually explode this very night, although astronomers do not expect this to happen for several billion years.

Now the pioneer of twentieth-century analytical philosophy was of course well aware that the rising of the sun is not a *scientific image*, but only our *manifest image* (Wilfrid Sellars) of what in truth is an entirely different state of affairs. An alternative reading of the sentence – reading between the lines, and admittedly a bit skewed in its banality – would then be: What if tomorrow the sun *actually* rises (which, as we *know*, has never happened before)?

It is slowly dawning on us what Wittgenstein wanted to say with this message in a bottle, some hundred years after he wrote it down in an Italian military prison in 1918. Statement 6.36311 of the *Tractatus* heralds a world in which it is possible both that the sun will come up tomorrow and that it will not come up. As Wolfram Eilenberger[8] polemicized in his recent book on philosophy's golden decade, it is symptomatic that precisely the founding father of almost fanatically anti-metaphysical logical positivism undertook such a fundamental critique – although one consistently ignored by his academic disciples – of the articles of faith of scientifically enlightened modernity.

It may be, however, that modernity's error goes well beyond its failure to distinguish between "logical necessity" and "nomological necessity." The delusion of many natural scientists (not natural science itself), along with their apologists, who now dominate philosophical institutions worldwide, lies not simply in their desire to explain anything and everything in causal terms, but perhaps in their faith in eternally immutable natural laws.

A NEW AGE REQUIRES NEW NATURAL LAWS – If we look back at the history of utopian novels beginning in 1516 with Thomas More's *Utopia* (full title: *On the Best State of a Republic and the New Island Utopia*), we find that, influenced by the discovery of completely new territories and the so-called New World, they initially described journeys to foreign places. It was not until much later that these spatial utopias were joined by temporal utopias existing in some other time.

Keen observers of – often dystopian – science-fiction films have noticed a further shift in recent years. The classics of the genre, from Stanley Kubrick to Andrei Tarkovsky to Ridley Scott, toil away at a universe governed by natural laws, one that for all the unfathomability of the theory of relativity yet maintains its physical contours. As Dietmar Dath notes, however, in more recent films such as Shane Carruth's *Upstream Color* (2013) and Dennis Villeneuve's *Arrival* (2016), the old speculative fiction inspired by Einstein has given way to something more Darwinian: "Everything, including how we perceive space (in Carruth) and time (in Villeneuve), is subject to the determinations of evolution or natural history. Even physical laws are locked in perpetual struggle with each other like competing genes. The universe contains nothing but mutation, variation, selection."[9]

Physical certitudes were already becoming increasingly (im)probable a century ago with the discovery of the uncertainty principle in quantum physics. As Rupert Sheldrake writes, "In the twentieth century it became clear that not just quantum processes but almost all natural phenomena are probabilistic, including the turbulent flow of liquids, the breaking of waves on the seashore, and the weather: they show a spontaneity and indeterminism that eludes exact prediction."[10] The speculative philosopher and mathematician Alfred North Whitehead came to an even more radical conclusion: "People make the mistake of talking about 'natural laws.' There *are* no natural laws. There are only temporary habits of nature."[11] But what does it mean for an age when it becomes estranged from its own natural laws or loses them entirely?

THE ORIGIN OF A NEW AGE – What does it mean for a society when the meaning of its metaphysically or scientifically established concepts changes, and not imperceptibly over generations, but within just a few years, in a way that is noticeable in the lives of individuals?

We are living in such an age, when not only things are changing, but time itself. Walter Benjamin's concept of origin is helpful in this context: "Origin, although an entirely historical category, has, nevertheless, nothing to do with genesis. The term origin is not intended to describe the process by which the existent came into being, but rather to describe that which emerges from the process of becoming and disappearance. Origin is an eddy in the stream of becoming, and in its current it swallows the material involved in the process of genesis."[12] We are not experiencing simply this or that new event, but the advent of a new age. What we lack, and what alone can help us to understand this new age, are new concepts and a revision of the originally metaphysical concepts and central categories of philosophy that we already possess. A *future metaphysics.*

Substance/Accident

AN INSCRUTABLE GRIN – Substance and accident not only have been central concepts of metaphysics since antiquity, but also – like so many other philosophical distinctions – have found their way, entirely unnoticed, into our everyday thinking. We constantly think of this or that as substantial, i.e. central and important, the other as accidental and negligible.

Traditionally, substance (from the Latin *substare*, to stand underneath) is that which underlies everything. That which could be excluded without changing the essence of something is accident (in Latin: *accidens*). The essence of a house, for example, includes the walls and roof that constitute a space more or less protected from the influences of the outside world. The color of the façade and the number of windows – or indeed, strictly speaking, whether or not there are any windows at all – are, by contrast, minor details. A human being must have a head, while a face is composed of eyes, nose, and mouth – whether the latter is smiling or not is irrelevant. Whoever would make such a claim, however, has probably never fallen for someone else's smile, and in their sheer contemplation has forgotten that a person's smile is by no means insignificant, but something that cannot be imagined away.

And then there is the Cheshire Cat from Lewis Carroll's *Alice's Adventures in Wonderland*, that grinning feline whose mouth we still see even after he has made himself disappear, compelling us to ask what is essential to a thing and what only incidental – or, in the terminology established over the history of philosophy: what the *hypo-keimenon* (Greek: "that which underlies") or *sub-stantia* (Latin: "that which stands underneath") is when we no longer look upon it as an opposing "surface" that fascinates us. Good to know that a smile or a look is sometimes enough to turn an entire philosophical construct into a glass house.

WHEN ONE THING NO LONGER FOLLOWS THE OTHER – We are used to the idea that one thing follows another, that things take their course and events play out as the laws of nature dictate. And naturally in everyday life we know what can be traced back to what. The stain on my pants is from my morning coffee, or actually from the man at the buffet who bumped into me, or strictly speaking from the cup spilling over in my hand that couldn't move away in time.

Aristotle and the medieval scholastics who followed him recognized four types of causes: formal causes (materials can take on different colors); material causes (brown liquids leave brown stains on white pants); efficient or moving causes (someone bumps into me and my hand moves); and lastly – as we can see even with respect to such a trivial matter as the discoloration of white summer trousers – final causes (mishaps occur that cannot be said to have any purpose or significance, even when we consider them from all logically possible perspectives).

With every large-scale catastrophe – the sinking of the Titanic, say – a shocked public once again asks itself the same much debated questions: was the disaster caused by a higher power, human negligence, or a technical malfunction? Was the ship fated to hit the iceberg? Was the captain at fault? Or was the death toll so high simply because there weren't enough lifeboats and help didn't arrive quickly enough?

In addition to such more or less straightforward misfortunes, we also have to deal with so-called "wicked problems" whose complexity makes it impossible to distinguish strictly between cause and effect, a precondition of traditional determinations of causality. It is only for this reason that (particularly legal) debates over whether smoking actually causes cancer, or whether a warming climate can be traced back directly to the use of carbon-based fuels, can drag on for decades (thanks to clever attorneys, and in the interest of lobbyists).

Advanced approaches in quantum physics or chaos theory have long since abandoned the question, virulent since the days of Newton, of whether everything that occurs can be explained by fundamentally mechanical causes. Numerous skeptics throughout the history of philosophy, most prominently perhaps David Hume in the eighteenth century, have even disavowed all forms of causality or necessity in the spirit of empiricism. Contemporary efforts by speculative materialists to smash the Gordian knot of causality by no longer admitting any necessity other than that of absolute contingency are perhaps even more radical, a risky intellectual maneuver in a risky age.

SUBSTANTIAL ACCIDENTS – A look at the dominant technologies of the twenty-first century suggests a more common definition of the word "accident." In the sense of unexpected calamities or misfortunes, accidents have a different relationship to the substance that underlies them. No longer mere accessories to substance, twenty-first-century accidents have the potential to turn the existing (metaphysical) order upside down. The catastrophes that threaten us today are not merely accidental in the Aristotelian sense, i.e. they do not concern only partial aspects, but threaten the system in question as a whole. This applies not only to a potential nuclear disaster, but also to the "glitches" of the financial world or the looming collapse of the climate. "We have witnessed the emergence of the algorithmic catastrophe that must be distinguished from industrial or military accidents. The causality of an industrial accident could be traced and avoided, but the control of algorithmic catastrophe is increasingly beyond the capacity of human beings."[13] So writes the philosopher of technology Yuk Hui, who further asserts that "[a]ll catastrophes are algorithmic, even the natural ones."[14]

Algorithmic or cybernetic catastrophes pose fundamentally new questions for metaphysics. (At the end of his life, faced with cybernetics as a science for regulating and controlling complex social organizations, living organisms, and machines, Heidegger even prematurely prophesied the end of metaphysics itself.) Certainly not the least important of these is whether it is possible to use advanced technologies to get a grip on anthropogenic problems (i.e. problems that we ourselves have created), or whether we are now dealing with "runaway technologies" that are racing away from us, and from the problems they have created, *for good.*

ALGORITHMIC UNPREDICTABILITY – What does the phrase "runaway technology" actually mean? One possible reading is that algorithms, for example, are capable of generating unpredictabilities in accordance with their fixed structure. Interestingly, this phenomenon is often identified by (mostly male) philosophers of technology as having catastrophic potential.

Luciana Parisi suggests a more positive reading of algorithmically generated unpredictabilities, based on the assumption that "the computational searching for the incomputable space of nondenumerable quantities has become superior to the view that algorithms are simply instructions leading to optimized solutions."[15] This incomputable space is not simply a negatively infinite sequence, but rather constitutes a substantial unpredictability; in establishing this space, algorithms have an effect on our existence. In the twenty-first century, then, we are dealing not primarily with unpredictable catastrophism, but with the opening up of promising potentialities of communication and coordination. Algorithms so understood would then be a kind of "runaway technology" racing toward a new, positive (metaphysical) infinity.

HOMO NARRANS VS. *HOMO APOCALYPTICUS* – One of the countless definitions of what human beings are or may be is that we are storytelling animals, meaning that we understand every development in terms of its end. *All's well that ends well*, so *don't count your chickens before they've hatched*. This is particularly true of modern human beings – "Kummt eh da Komet!" (*The comet is coming anyway!*), the Austrian folk poet Johann Nestroy once wrote, to the reassurance of his morbid nineteenth-century audience. Perhaps this is one reason why we seem so unconcerned by the *sixth* (and possibly final) *great extinction* that we ourselves are in the midst of bringing about.

"The problem," as Jean-Pierre Dupuy writes, "is that catastrophe is not believable: it is held to be possible only once it has occurred, and by that point it is too late. This obstacle can be overcome, I believe, only if an utterly new metaphysical conception is adopted of our relationship to time."[16] This has been particularly true for the past two centuries. According to Bruno Latour, "Modernity is living entirely within the Apocalypse or, more precisely, as we shall soon see, *after* the Apocalypse. This is why modernity has condemned itself to understanding nothing about what history is bringing it that is really new. So, we have to agree finally to engage for real in an apocalyptic discourse *in the present time*."[17]

Secularized thought plays its post-apocalyptic game as though time were already at an end, the Last Judgment already delivered. But can we also integrate the apocalypse philosophically into our thinking, other than as ushering us, like Nietzsche's "last man," squinting into the end of history? In his book *Nihil Unbound*, the philosopher Ray Brassier – who against his own wishes has since been branded a speculative realist – espouses the idea of a radicalized, progressive, speculative nihilism. Of course, we are all already dead, the sun has exploded, i.e. we know all about the collapse of anything and everything, the complete disappearance not only of this author and his readers, but of every recording medium and every sign that might attest to our existence. But apocalyptic thought is not simply about the idea that, from the perspective of such a future, we may as well never have existed, insofar as nothing and no one will be able to decipher any trace of our existence. *Apocalypse* (from the Greek *apokalypsis*, meaning "revelation" or "unveiling") means first and foremost a historical "turning point". In this sense, apocalyptic thought is not catastrophic thought, but rather, in formal terms, allows us to look back from the future onto the past, which includes our own present.

Thinking apocalyptically thus means not celebrating catastrophe, but changing our goals and our conception of the direction of time. The solution is not catastrophism, but anastrophism (from the Greek *anastrephein*, "to turn back"). An inversion of time and time for new thinking.

ON THE NATURAL POLITICAL QUESTION OF WHETHER THERE EVER WILL HAVE BEEN NATURAL LAWS – The idea that we exist in a world without natural laws in which time passes counterintuitively, or in a world in which natural laws are constantly changing, is unsettling. And yet skeptical philosophers regularly set out to expose at least the regularity of nature as a metaphysical hypostatization. This would mean that natural laws are due only to our habit, and that no matter how often events have repeatedly occurred in the past, this does not imply that nature will continue to remain reliable indefinitely into the future. Things that are considered impossible today might become everyday occurrences tomorrow, just as a statement that was false yesterday may turn out to be true at some later date.

We are dealing here with fundamental philosophical questions of time. Up to now, we could either assume, in accordance with traditional metaphysics, that (the laws of) the future will be the same as (those of) the past, or, following the skeptics, that the laws of nature might change in the future. In the twenty-first century, however, we can and must conceive of a third option, namely, that past and future *cannot* be the same at all. Intervening in the midst of the millennia-old reasoning that laws empirically demonstrated in the present will in the future either change or remain the same, we now have the speculative suggestion that their continued existence is ultimately contingent. Or, in the words of the speculative materialist Quentin Meillassoux: "I posit that there is no Universe of universes of cases; I posit that time can bring forth any non-contradictory set of possibilities. As a result, I accord to time the capacity to bring forth new laws which were not 'potentially' contained in some fixed set of possibles; I accord to time the capacity to bring forth situations *which were not at all contained in precedent situations.*"[18]

Once freed from the chrono-logical constraints of natural laws, we see that there are also other possible objections relating to time. Need we speak of a potential nullification of natural *laws* at all? Perhaps these laws are, strictly speaking, rather systems that never concern the whole of infinity, but only part of it or a partial set of axioms, and within which relations are formed that allow different "laws" to operate. In a spaceship, for example, the "laws" of gravity are practically inoperative, and instead of describing the burning of an object as a causal relationship, we could also conceive of it as a relational shift within a system, a change within a relation between part and whole (a molecule disintegrates, oxygen atoms are bound together, etc.).

Just as laws are valid or in force only within the framework of a certain politics, gravity is not experienceable in a spaceship orbiting the earth (as though it did not exist at all). Laws are always part of a certain politics and lose their physical evidence outside of their territory. Without mobilizing a new (or old) form of relativism against the natural sciences, we can say in the face of such meta-physical doubt that natural laws are always part of a politics of nature.

SLIM CHANCE FOR CHANCE – Society and cultural structures are commonly understood as preventative mechanisms meant to defend against caprice and lawlessness. We, moreover, live in a culture that essentially seeks to defend against the incursion of the unexpected. To this end, we have not only laws to be followed under threat of punishment, but even distinct cognitive categories of necessity and legality.

Our social, political, and metaphysical thought has made itself comfortable with these categories. And where this has no longer been possible in the modern era, we have proven to be ingenious at creating other categories. The invention of chance (*hazard*, from the Arabic *az-zahr*, meaning "token" or "game piece") or aleatorics (from the Latin *alea*, meaning "dice") serves the comforting illusion that we can tame the uncontrollable by ascribing to unexpected events, if not a divine subject to be prayed to, then at least a numerically or mathematically manageable risk. The idea behind this is that the incalculable can be rationally controlled – a fantasy that nonetheless "makes sense," i.e. that can have reality creating effects, as in the insurance industry.

"The belief in chance," Meillassoux explains, "is inevitably a metaphysical belief, since it incorporates the belief in the factual necessity of determinate probabilistic laws, which it is no longer possible to account for except via the necessity of supposed deterministic laws."[19] A future metaphysics for the twenty-first century will not be able to content itself with the forced application of probability theory to phenomena that are ultimately contingent. From this perspective, attempts to explain or idealize radical contingency as chance or as the occurrence of an improbability appear as efforts to normalize a stochastics that indulges in fantasies of omnipotence. The probabilistic palette ranges from one-sided drone warfare, with its promise of minimizing casualties (at least on the side of "liberal" societies, from whom media reports now expect low casualty rates, regardless of how high the price for this is on the other side), to romantic relationships that involve minimal risks because they have been prescreened by optimizing algorithms. What is suppressed here are not only other kinds of warfare and relationships, but the entire idea of the Other defined precisely by its incalculability. But shouldn't the exact opposite, i.e. contact with the unknown as well as knowing what we do not know (and cannot control), be a gauge of progressivity?

AB-NORMALITIES, OR WHEN THE EXCEPTIONS ARE
MORE CONSISTENT THAN THE RULE – In the age
of the algorithm, misfortunes that were once
accidental have become substantial. In various
and diverse fields, we observe anomalies that
have mutated to become (ab-)normal, bringing
a proper measure of instability to cybernetic systems (including those of social control) that were
once famed for their ability to create order.

This goes well beyond the idea of the "glitch"
as a mode of accelerated production, celebrated
in Silicon Valley circles under the motto "Move
fast and break things." As Jussi Parikka and Tony
D. Sampson write, "In practice, the programs
written by hackers, spammers, virus writers,
and those pornographers intent on redirecting
our browsers to their content, have problematized the intended functionality and deployment
of cybernetic systems."[20] If up to 40 percent of
all the e-mails we are now bombarded with are
spam – bringing with them pornographic content, viruses, etc. – then we can hardly speak
here of anomalies (in the sense of more or less
insignificant deviations from the norm). Dealing
with spam – setting up mail filters, employing
virus scanners, activating pop-up ad blockers,

etc. – has become a "normal" part of using the internet, an ab-normality.

Just as spam and computer viruses are part of our everyday digital life, we must also understand the high-frequency derivative economy – which operates under the paradigm of the digital – in terms of its "glitches" (just as we must understand our politics in terms of the supposed anomaly of the refugee). We are dealing here not with black sheep or Nassim Taleb's black swans, i.e. not with more or less improbable extreme events, but with what the volatility trader and market metaphysician Elie Ayache describes in his book *The Blank Swan: The End of Probability* as a new normality. Abnormality.

THINKING IN TERMS OF NEW PATHOLOGIES – Artists and philosophers (especially male ones) have always thought of themselves as exemplifying that which elevates human beings above the rest of creation. And they have linked this precisely to their suffering, traditionally to their melancholia, and more recently preferably to a sense of being existentially thrown into the absurdity of being or nothingness. The loss of traditional meaning, the fear of losing one's voice or even language itself in the face of rapid change, are signs of a depressive condition, symptoms of suffering from an inability to realize one's own potential, individually as well as socially or politically.

The leftist theorist Franco Berardi understands depression as "a condition close to the Truth because it is the moment in which we grasp the non-existence of meaning."[21] It may well be that, today and in the future, what opens our eyes to the great and true questions are not particularly distinctive moments in our own individual existence, but rather the quotidian banality of the catastrophes and pathologies that affect us all. We are afflicted with a twenty-first-century syndrome that with the advent of the internet, social media, and corresponding smart devices has bestowed upon us a series of new pathologies. Contemporary "iDisorders," to use Larry Rosen's term,[22] are distinct from the neurotic and hysterical ailments and paralyses popular at the beginning of the previous century as well as from the allergies that flourished at its end: attention deficit disorders, narcissistic personality disorders, insomnia, obsessive-compulsive disorders including the constant checking of e-mails or social media (along with the social anxieties they catalyze), hallucinatory perceptions such as the imagined vibrating or ringing of one's smartphone, and many more.

The corresponding pathologies have been attributed to a variety of causes, including individual chemical/biological imbalances under *narco-capitalism* (Laurent de Sutter), *pharmaco-pornographic biocapitalism* (Paul Preciado), and the neoliberal transition from Fordist to post-Fordist labor conditions (Jon Lindblom). With a view toward recent research on the plasticity of the human brain and the notion of an "ontology of the accident," Catherine Malabou's approach is particularly interesting, not least because of her polemical turn against the established metaphysical or biological distinction between brain and mind or between neurological and psychiatric problems. "It must be stated outright," she writes: "No philosopher has ever approached the immense problem of cerebral suffering" in a way "that would be at once epistemological, clinical, and metaphysical."[23]

In the new metabiology and metapsychiatry of the twenty-first century, the boundary between organic and sociopolitical traumas has become permeable. Here, too, we are dealing not with accidental anomalies, but with significant and substantial abnormalities, including not only the effects of spectacular head injuries (brain traumas, lesions), but also the everyday effects of brains that are growing ever older. The old metaphysical questions about personal identity are thus posed again in new ways. Instead of the abstract query, "Is one responsible for an action that one does not remember?", we now ask, "Is my grandmother suffering from Alzheimer's disease still the same person, or has she become someone else?" As Malabou writes, "The accidents of cerebrality are wounds that cut the thread of history, place history outside itself, suspend its course, and remain hermeneutically 'irrecoverable' even though the psyche remains alive. *The cerebral accident thus reveals the ability of the subject to survive the senselessness of its own accidents.*"[24] We are and become the creations of what befalls us, creatures of our own accidents, which are anything but trivial matters. Or, to modify Kant's famous definition: Enlightenment in the third millennium means humanity's emergence from our self-imposed ignorance of the substantial accidentality of our existence.

Form/Matter

DECONSTRUCTIVE NANOTECHNOLOGY: WELL-INFORMED FORMS OF MATTER – It became an established belief in the second half of the last century that the task of critical thought or critical art lies in deconstructing traditional metaphysical distinctions like substance/accident, form/content, or body/mind. (First coined by Jacques Derrida, the term "deconstruction" – like the philosophical concepts of "substance," "mind," and "form" before it – is on the point of becoming an often misused part of everyday speech.) Feminists pointed out the patriarchal structure of dualisms like the opposition of active, masculine-coded form and passive, feminine-coded matter, a word that goes back to the Latin *materia*, itself derived from *mater* (mother) as a compelling translation of the Greek *physis*. Such "occidental" distinctions and divisions were also challenged from a postcolonial perspective. And there are in fact often residues here of a "Western" dominance that, not least for geopolitical reasons, has since lost its hegemonic power and persuasiveness.

Even setting aside any and all political, artistic, or other categories of critique, the relation between form and matter has also been transformed on the terrain of scientific rationality. Advances in the field of nanotechnology, for example, have shown that the materiality or "material" substance of an object is mutable. (With the insight that matter itself can be deconstructed, nanotechnology is in a way "following" the path indicated by French poststructuralism.)

What we inadequately describe as molding or changing the shape of materials – here, too, we are in need of a new philosophical language – is in fact an intervention into the structure of matter itself. In the age of nanotechnology, when we know that altering a material affects not only its external form, but also its substance, the metaphysical categories that once defined our culture and art are also becoming problematic.

A future metaphysics informed by nanotechnology moreover provides a reasonable basis for understanding matter itself as information that communicates with itself, as Friedrich Kittler concluded with fierce consistency. Machines, and perhaps even technology in general, are accordingly no longer merely tools for human beings, but are themselves intelligent feedback mechanisms with which matter comes to know itself in crystalline quantum dimensions. This further corresponds with our understanding of our own biological nature as being packed with information, i.e. with understanding DNA as a carrier of genetic information and the material basis of our genes. Thus the metaphysical premise underlying all quantum physics or gene technology is the insight that our material nature is always already more than mere *physis*. Metaphysis.

ENDURING APPEAL OF DUALISMS – Who can help but crack a pitying smile over all the attempts throughout the history of philosophy to demonstrate the divine origin of human reason or the independence of the human mind from all earthly phenomena? And what were the materialist heretics of philosophy even thinking, being banished or, like Giordano Bruno, even burned at the stake for their antireligious views?

The fact that even today philosophers continue to engage in endless debates over free will or whether our decisions are neurophysiologically determined would consequently be nothing other than spleen or the result of professional deformation. The same could also be said of the enthusiasm shown for recent philosophical approaches like *psychophysical parallelism* or *dualistic interactionism*, which are ultimately only reformulations of approaches first described centuries ago by philosophers like Baruch Spinoza.

But has the anti-metaphysical pragmatism so prevalent today actually advanced any further than what came before it? How do we respond when someone tells us about their constantly shifting allergies or chronic feelings of depression? Do we not then tend to fall back on long-familiar reflexes and reactions when we advise them to take medication or go to a psychoanalyst – or (and this is the third philosophical option) when we bring out the magic word "psychosomatic," which is nothing other than a mystic code word for an interdependence of mind and body that is not even rudimentarily understood but merely asserted?

It seems as though we armchair metaphysicians still have not overcome certain antiquated dualisms. Behind our recommendation to give talk therapy a try lurks a belief that the mental is independent of the physical, or – even worse – an implicit assumption of free will. And behind our advice to reach for antidepressants when psychological or psychoanalytic treatment no longer helps is the deterministic admission that everything ultimately comes down to one's physical (pre)disposition. Only with great effort will we be able to, if not liberate ourselves from the dualisms that shape our culture, at least constructively think further with them than before.

THEOLOGY OF DEMATERIALIZATION – There is no thinking outside metaphysics, no non-metaphysical thought. Instead there is a lot of bad or imprecise philosophical thinking, not only from professional academic philosophers, but also and especially wherever metaphysical categories remain implicit and unreflected upon.

As an example of the latter, consider the many debates over digital technologies, which even in their choice of terminology betray suspicious metaphysical presuppositions. "Network" and, even more so, "cloud" are two such deceptive or ideological concepts that obscure the material basis of all computation. N. Katherine Hayles has written a book about "how information lost its body" (*How We Became Posthuman*), and Ed Finn has noted that "the fact that algorithms must always be implemented to be used is actually their most significant feature. By occupying and defining that awkward middle ground, algorithms and their human collaborators enact new roles as culture machines that unite ideology and practice, pure mathematics and impure humanity, logic and desire."[25]

All too often, however, the material platforms and materials used are concealed, as though there were such a thing as pure software without hardware. A compulsion to repeat antiquated metaphysical dualisms, not least that of form vs. content or mind vs. matter, can be observed wherever the current state of technology is not accompanied by an appropriate level of philosophical reflection. We know the tendency in philosophy to eliminate anything material – there is of course also the reverse exclusion mechanism, with hardened materialists ruling out the significance of any and all immaterial or

mental components – as "idealism," beginning
with Plato, but especially with the Neoplatonists
(such as Plotinus), for whom all life (including
material life) resulted from mental ideas. And
today, numerous ideologues of the *algo-cathedral*
(Ian Bogost), whose spiritual fervor (for data)
is scarcely less intense than that of medieval
theologians, are repeating the very same idealistic
symptoms without knowing it.

"Overlooking" the material aspects of new
technology is especially convenient for those
who profit from the underlying material relations
of power and exploitation. (The clearest objection comes from Friedrich Kittler, who several
decades ago declared that *there is no software*.)
What was true centuries ago – in the ancient
slaveholder society of Athens or in the religious
Middle Ages – remains true in the age of neo-
feudalistic monopoly capitalism under Google,
Facebook, Amazon, and co.: our ignorance with
respect to the material foundations of the "cloud"
or to what is misguidedly called *immaterial labor*
not only burdens every individual, but affects
our society as a whole. Digital platforms, too,
are only possible qua the exploitation of material resources: of nature (silicon for microchips,

cobalt for lithium-ion batteries, etc.), of the physis of the people who dismantle, assemble, and install them, and finally of all those who use and consume them.

The ideology of immateriality or dematerialization is armchair philosophy in the service of those who currently rule. Here, as everywhere else, there is a connection between what is metaphysically wrong and what is politically wrong. Bad metaphysics always serves bad politics.

Life/Death

PHILOSOPHY'S SLEEP BEARS SCIENTIFIC MONSTERS – It is no coincidence that vampire stories emerged in literature at the dawn of the nineteenth century and proceeded to spread like an epidemic. The literary figure of the vampire was itself a revenant, its emergence an eerie return of those "real" vampire epidemics that had occurred several decades earlier primarily along the eastern border of the Habsburg empire.

The vampire is distinguished by its refusal to resign itself to death, instead returning to life again and again by drinking the blood of the living. It thus confuses the polarization of body and soul, material and form, passivity and activity, distinctions consistently posited as

ontological throughout the history of philosophy. This makes it the paradigmatic incarnation
of a new questioning of the boundary between
life and death, a monster both metaphysical and
scientific.

Vampires embody in an exemplary way the
principles of life as they were reconceived around
1800. Or put another way, they haunt precisely
the scientific order that was establishing itself at
the same time. It is no coincidence that modern
biology, which set out to precisely define life and
death and thus isolate them from each other for
the first time, emerged at exactly the same time
as the historical vampire epidemics. If previously
"biology was unknown," first materializing only
around this time, there was, as Michel Foucault
writes, "a very simple reason for [this]: that life
itself did not exist. All that existed was living
beings, which were viewed through a grid of
knowledge constituted by *natural history*."[26]

The invention of the discipline of biology (as
the science of life) and its new object did not
explain life itself, however, but rather first made
it a problem. Scientific inquiry into life itself and
the insight that life cannot be strictly isolated
from death have gone hand in hand from the

beginning, even up to more recent definitions advanced by the likes of John Maynard Smith and Eörs Szathmáry, according to whom anything is "alive" that is passed down with mutations and is subject to evolution via natural selection. (Gregory Chaitin captures this in the lovely equation *life = randomly evolving software.*)[27]

Most "explanations," such as the physicist Ernst Schrödinger's definition that something is alive if it takes in energy from and excretes waste back into its environment by means of a stored program, raise more questions than they answer. According to the chemist James Lovelock, life is possible only if it is carbon-based (i.e. also on the basis of silicon-based carriers of information). Even the biological criterion of reproductive capacity serves mainly to generate further metaphysical confusion, as it excludes not only highly active entities like viruses, but also – sophistically exaggerated – post-menopausal women and impotent men.

"Life" as such has never been discovered, and as a ready object for individual sciences is nowhere to be found. Rather, biology, no less than chemistry and physics, itself raises the very metaphysical questions that we believe it to answer.

HAUNTOLOGY, OR HOW VAMPIRES HAUNT PHI-
LOSOPHY AND SCIENCE – Although he never
wrote anything about it directly, Immanuel Kant
– perhaps the most important philosopher of the
last two centuries – has been dubbed *the* philosopher of vampirism by Slavoj Žižek. Throughout
his life, Kant grappled with problems adjacent
to the vampire epidemics of which he was a contemporary, and particularly with his three great
Critiques of the 1780s, he took it upon himself to
tame a metaphysically overtaxed spirit.

But already in 1766, in *Dreams of a Spirit-Seer
Elucidated through Dreams of Metaphysics*, Kant
had attempted a critical self-reflection of his own
intellectual limits as well as of the rationalistic
psychology of his age. Nearly two decades before
his epochal *Critique of Pure Reason*, he saw this
as the completion of his critical work (from the
Greek *krinein*, "to draw boundaries"), writing
that "perhaps in the future there can be all sorts
of *opinions* [about spiritual beings] but never any
[more] *knowledge* about them."[28] *Dreams of a
Spirit-Seer* seeks to establish an epistemological
distinction between ghosts and spiritual beings,
as "the philosophical concept of spiritual being[s]
[…] is completely different. It can be completed

but understood *negatively*, namely, by fixing securely the limits of our insight and convincing us that the various appearances of *life* in nature and their laws are all that is granted to us to know, but the principle of this life, i.e., spiritual nature, which one cannot know but rather [only] suppose, can never be positively thought."[29]

Kant once again took up the theme of *negation*, so important to the superhuman or inhuman logic of the life principles of the vampire, in his *Critique of Pure Reason*. There he elaborated a *transcendental logic* (transcendental here in the sense of defining the conditions of the possibility of knowledge) that recognizes, in addition to *negative* and *positive judgments*, what he calls *infinite judgments*. His resumption of this theme can be brought into direct connection with the questions about life and death posed by the theory of the vampire, as the example he uses to illustrate the necessity of an infinite judgment is, tellingly, the question of the mortality of the body or of the immortality of the soul that haunts both biology and metaphysics. In the case of a simple positive judgment, the answer to the latter question is *no* (the soul is mortal); in the case of a negative judgment, *yes* (the soul is immortal). Speculative dissatisfaction with both answers leads Kant to expand formal Aristotelian (onto-)logic and posit an infinite judgment about what he calls the "undying" or "non-mortal."

Being or nonbeing, life or death, the mortality or immortality of the soul or spirit – all of these themes regrouped around 1800 in the fields of critical philosophy and natural science. At issue were the well-trodden metaphysical and onto-logical questions about being and nonbeing per se, along with questions about the ambiguous modal status of metaphysics itself: Does it exist? Should it (rather not) exist? Questions about life and death, being and nonbeing, haunt not only philosophy, but also the natural sciences. Metaphysics, so understood, is more than ontol-ogy; it is, as Derrida once called it, hauntology.

PHILOSOPHY AS LEARNING TO DIE – In contrast to wisdom teachings and religious creeds that focus on advice for achieving bliss or eternal life, classical philosophy exhibits a striking preoccu-pation with death. *To study philosophy is to learn to die*, as one oft-quoted definition has it. This fits with the frequently expressed modern complaint that, living under increasingly anonymized and alienated metropolitan conditions – and despite or perhaps precisely because of the advances of modern medicine – we have forgotten what it means to die humanely and with dignity.

In an age when our entire species is under threat, these definitions must be expanded and radicalized without any civilization-weary nostalgia. This applies particularly to the (at least since Heidegger) classic existentialist trope that every individual dies alone and no one can save us from death, a notion that requires reinterpretation in light of the *sixth great extinction* of the Anthropocene, which may well yet threaten its own perpetrators (who in Germany alone slaughter nearly 800 million animals every year). Death, annihilation, and extinction are no longer only individual events. We are confronted with the question of our responsibility to other species and the planet as a whole. *Geontological* questions about the relation between being and earth thus take on new meaning. "As the future of human life – or a human way of life – is put under pressure from the heating of the planet, ontology has reemerged as a central problem in philosophy, anthropology, literary and cultural studies, and in science and technology studies," as Elizabeth A. Povinelli describes the "struggle to maintain a difference that makes a difference between all forms of Life and the category of Nonlife."[30]

While the seemingly inextinguishable, undead fantasy of human immortality is currently receiving a new techno-utopian boost, a new mental horizon is opening up alongside it, namely, that it is high time to start conceiving of a world without human beings. There are moreover good reasons to believe that the (for the most part implicit) assumption that the continued existence of our species is tied to that of the planet has been nothing more than an optimistic illusion. What if saving the planet and saving the human race are not parallel processes? For even if we were to actually decide not to continue systematically destroying the earth, this would not even come close to guaranteeing the survival of our species. And have we even decided whether "our survival" means all of us, all seven (and soon to be ten) billion of our fellow inhabitants, or only the human race as such? And what would it mean – philosophically, no less than socially or politically – if these options were mutually exclusive, as suggested by the political and environmental movement of "denatalism," which advocates for a radical reduction in birth rates? Or the Voluntary Human Extinction Movement …

POST-/TRANS-/INHUMAN: WHAT WILL WE HAVE BEEN? – We do not even want to imagine life without artificial aids. Without glasses, we would stumble around half blind, and death rates would rapidly skyrocket simply in the absence of pacemakers firmly implanted in the human body or other similar technical devices. And is there anyone – apart from a handful of religious freaks and esotericists who rail against vaccinations and birth control pills – who thinks that starting hormone therapy means the beginning of the end of a human existence?

Are we not at some point crossing a line, however, when our biology – here understood as always already *post*humanist – is simply overloaded with too much technology, or when our sperm and egg cells are subject to genetic manipulation? Such interventions would imply inheritable changes and could make human beings into longer-lasting design objects, if not lead to the eternal life dreamt of by *trans*humanists.

It is doubtful that such quantitative categories, or categories operating with a temporal before and after, will move us forward either philosophically or socially. Attempting to measure just how much technology a human being can absorb without losing his or her humanity reduces our intellectual horizon. The question of at what point we are (finally) no longer human – whether presented as a horror scenario or a wishful fantasy – generally falls short. Posthumanists and transhumanists alike ultimately err at a fundamental level, namely that of a philosophy of time. For all their other differences and internal contradictions, they share a temporal model that could be divided into a *before* human beings and an *after*: human life made permanent thanks to medical advances, a perpetual human mind that transcends biological limits, whose thoughts and memories would be stored for eternity on (presumably maintenance-free) hard drives.

The concept of the inhuman posited by speculative, accelerationist, and xenofeminist philosophers is distinguished from such post- or transhumanist fantasies first by its more complex temporal structure. Always already inhuman human beings cannot be understood in terms of some natural essence defined in the past, but only in terms of our future. With every artificial invention of our intelligence – indeed every time we make use of our rationality and intellect – the idea, self-conception, and essence of what it means to be human also changes. There is no human being, but only human becoming.

TECHNOPHOBIA AND FEAR OF ARTIFICIAL AMNESIA – The first great philosophical writer, Plato, railed against the medium of writing as a danger not only to philosophy, but to the human mind itself. Specifically, the theory is that writing goes hand in hand with memory loss or loss of our "natural" capacity for memory. The more we write down, the less we have to remember; the more we record, the more we forget.

Such concerns underestimate the astonishing plasticity of the human brain. Neurological studies show not so much a loss of as a shift in the relevant brain functions: from content to the places where said content is to be found. We are constantly surrounded by smartphones and laptops on which we can at any time take down our thoughts or excerpt and save what we have just read or listened to, and which moreover allow us to access other online sources of knowledge whenever we want. Rather than storing information about all of the various topics and fields of knowledge that come at us, our brains naturally increasingly tend to recall what devices, paths, and technological sources we can use to call up information that we have previously found. Memory shift rather than memory loss.

The ancient and medieval mnemotechnics described by Frances Yates in *The Art of Memory* has thus become a *téchne* (Greek for "art, science, or technique") for taking recourse to artificial aids as efficiently as possible. But was not the ancient *ars memoriae* already an artistic and thus artificial technique? We have always sought to train our minds because we do not wish to content ourselves only with their naturally given capacities. Our eccentric brain has always existed outside of itself. As Michael Wheeler writes, "If our minds are partly in our smartphones and even in our buildings, then that is not a transformation in human nature, but only the latest manifestation of the age-old human ontology of dynamically assembled, organic-technological cognitive systems. Nevertheless, once our self-understanding catches up with our hybrid nature, the world promises to be a very different place."[31] Now we only need to get into our heads what has long been in our brains, i.e. what sort of changes take place there. Our brain itself is a plastic and as such artificial organ that reshapes itself in accordance with technological changes.

WHO'S AFRAID OF ARTIFICIAL INTELLIGENCE? – A strict separation between human beings and the animal realm is characteristic not only of the Christian tradition, but of (at least all monotheistic) religions in general. One of the most important criteria here is our intellect, long considered to be an exclusive trait of our species. Only human beings are supposed to be equipped with reason – whether by God, creation, or evolution – and as reasoning beings we are supposedly distinct from other animals, not to mention the rest of nature.

Regardless of whether or not this definition is correct, it is *de facto* the implicit or explicit justification of a millennia-old unscrupulousness that still persists today. It allows us to forget about the living conditions of the animals that we make use of or that are part of our food chain (wild animals make up only about four percent of mammalian biomass on earth; the other 96 percent are human beings and the livestock we breed and maintain), and it is probably also the reason that the extinction of numerous species ultimately seems to interest us as a species only when we ourselves are affected by it.

It is thus our (allegedly unique) intellect which has "justified" our absolute rule over and thoughtlessness toward non- or less intelligent life. And whether we are all aware of it or not, we are clearly afraid that an intelligence superior to ours would be even less natural or more hostile to nature than we are, and treat us lower beings even worse than we have treated less intelligent creatures.

NEVERENDING HUBRIS – Even in the face of its possible extinction, the human race opts for unrestrained hubris. No intelligence other than our own is supposed to exist. Intelligence is conceivable only in human terms – even if it is far superior to our own. This anthropocentric fixation, our inability to think past our own nose, as it were, can also be seen in the growing fear of artificial intelligence, or more specifically: of artificial human intelligence.

But is it not once again – one last time? – hubris to assume that an entirely different, nonhuman intelligence would have nothing better to do than concern itself with us, as though we were constantly busying ourselves with ants or sparrows? Is not, as Benjamin Bratton supposes, "the real nightmare, even worse than the one in which the big Machine wants to kill you, [...] the one in which it sees you as irrelevant, or not even as a discrete thing to know"?[32]

BIOMORPHIC CONFUSION – From an anthropocentric perspective, intelligence is ultimately not just a quality but even the sole property of human beings. All other intelligence is measured against human intelligence and thus appears either inferior or superior to it. This constricted point of view corresponds to a kind of biomorphic confusion that upon reflection appears as absurd as the first attempts at human flight using flexible airfoils or wings as seen in old film reels – as though humanity's age-old dream of flight could be fulfilled by imitating birds as closely as possible. Bratton reminds us that "biomorphic imitation is not how we design complex technology. Airplanes do not fly like birds fly, and we certainly do not try to trick birds into thinking that airplanes are birds in order to test whether those planes 'really' are flying machines. Why do it for AI then?"[33]

Although AI research with its new translation algorithms has since turned away from such attempts at biomorphic imitation, popular interest in the person of Alan Turing and the test bearing his name (an *imitation game*) testifies to a persistent misconception of the relation between ourselves and the machinic Other. This is not only a technological problem, but also has political consequences. For if we can understand the intelligence of the future only as artificially revamped human intelligence, then we are surrendering its potential to contribute to a future that will be something other than the present continuation of the past.

WHOSE INTELLIGENCE IS IT ANYWAY? – There is no lack of different definitions of intelligence. For the time being, however, consensus is nowhere in sight. Intelligent beings must, among other things, be able to act reasonably, to make independent judgments, to draft and execute plans, to communicate these plans to others in a natural language – the list could go on and on, without ever arriving at a final definition.

Another way of approaching these questions is to distinguish between different forms of human intelligence. According to Dirk Baecker, for example, human intelligence is highly complex, consisting of "mental intelligence, which is available to conscious thought; neural intelligence, through which the brain continuously produces and assesses images of its environment; and organic intelligence, through which the body maintains, moves, and conducts itself."[34] Now these definitions do not conform to a cohesive unity. Rather, there are a number of mutually contradictory overlappings, as well as open or unresolved areas. The parts turn out to form a whole that in turn is more than the sum of its parts. At the same time, the recursive whole is marked by gaps or holes that are more than just open spaces for the smoother interlocking of individual parts. Social and other kinds of intelligence are distinguished by a downright paradoxical ability to comprehend the incomprehensible, to calculate the incalculable, and to somehow integrate the incommensurable into one's own actions. We never know what makes others tick or what they will think of next. As though the ego were necessarily afraid both of the contingent intrusion of the alter ego and of itself, our collective egoism also reduces the potential for a different kind of mechanical or artificial intelligence.

We further misapprehend the machines that we ourselves have programmed. Such machines continue to be dependent on the data they are fed, which are by no means neutral, but always have human – all too human – proclivities. "Rise of the racist robots" reads the headline of a recent article in the *Guardian* on the racial biases of algorithms used by American prison administrations.[35] Analogous phenomena can be seen with respect to algorithms that judge male and female educators differently, or that make financial or legal decisions (for us). As is becoming ever clearer, actually existing forms of artificial intelligence have inherited the weaknesses of human thought, planning, and judgment.

Up to now, we have mostly encountered forms of mechanical intelligence that are inclined or even programmed to be able to dismiss, or rather ignore the forms of contingency and alterity described above. But what would an AI that could free itself (and us?) from the deficiencies of human thought, planning, and judgment be like?

A FASCINATING HISTORICAL CONSTELLATION, OR DOUBLE DECARBONIZATION – It is becoming more and more clear that a comprehensive decarbonization of both our industry and our everyday life is required if the fight against climate change is to have any chance of success. Decarbonization in this context – i.e. moving away from oil, gasoline, and plastic – is an aspirational goal meant to help ensure the survival of the human race. At the same time, however, a very different sort of decarbonization is emerging on the horizon that for some ominously heralds the disappearance of our carbon-based intellect in favor of the kind of silicon-based intelligence typical of our technological culture built on microchips. "We think we know quite a bit about animal intelligence and plant intelligence," Benjamin Bratton writes, "but AI at urban scale is for the most part a mineral intelligence. Metals, silica, plastics and information carved into them by electromagnetism form the material basis" of our future society.[36]

PHARMAKON SILICON – In his reflections on the medium of writing, Jacques Derrida comments extensively on the concept of the "pharmakon," which has since served others as a starting point for a general philosophy of technology. Writing, according to Derrida, is a pharmakon – at once both remedy and poison. And accordingly, every new technology is both the medium of a liberation and the threat of a new or even more comprehensive confinement.

The pharmakon is a diabolical instrument. Its double effect applies particularly to the resource silicon: on the one hand, one of the material preconditions of the digital revolution and its associated promise of human liberation, on the other, the medium and storage material for potential alternatives to human intelligence.

Carbon and silicon belong to the same group on the periodic table. Their tetravalent electron shells – with four active electrons in the outer shell – predestine them to combine with other elements like no other group. Hence according to some theorists, silicon, although it is a metal, even has the potential to behave like a living material. *Silicon Pharma*. Or inverting Hölderlin: where there is salvation, danger also grows.

BIOHYPERMEDIA AND THE LIBERATION OF TECH-
NOLOGY AND MAN – If we believe the reports
coming out of the most highly advanced robotics
laboratories at MIT, then in addition to silicon
components, organic tissue is increasingly in
demand for manufacturing the newest generation
of robots. The trend is toward such tissue becoming a component of future intelligent actors of
equal value to silicon and steel.

Beyond the changing uses of individual components in new contexts, this suggests first and
foremost a liberation of both technology and
human beings: emancipation from the strict
limits and definitions of the human as well as
from the obligation to continually produce new
objects (whether on Fordist assembly lines or
via post-Fordist automation). The technology
of the future will unfold directly on the human
body. *BioHypermedia* (Tiziana Terranova) and
biosemiosis (Benjamin Bratton) are the corresponding catchwords. Even in the "liberation" of
their respective potential, technology and human
beings seem to be bound together.

Changing Times

If I am right, the whole of our thinking about what we are, and what other people are, has to be restructured. This is not funny, and I do not know how long we have to do it.

Gregory Bateson

INTERGENERATIONAL POLITICS AND SLOW VIOLENCE – A suspicion is haunting us, the suspicion that our species simply isn't intelligent enough to confront the tasks which lie before us, i.e. to solve the problems facing society as a whole in the twenty-first century. To begin with, it is hopeless to try to address local problems divorced from their global contexts, which admittedly are only rarely recognizable as such in the here and now. But even apart from such paralyzing spatial challenges, there may also be even more important temporal complications, such as the overwhelming difficulty of intellectually processing developments that evolve exponentially rapidly, which would be the first precondition for developing long-term strategies in response to them. What Timothy Morton calls *hyperobjects* – which precisely are not present or contemporary, but rather phenomena such as climate change that are impossible to grasp as a whole – operate according to a new hypertemporality, or at any rate according to a temporality that structurally overwhelms us and our conception of time.

We are culturally and medially trained to react – if at all – only to concrete events that occur right before our eyes, and inured to anything that takes place below the threshold of dramatic attention or that does not assail us with sufficient media force. Largely overlooked and misunderstood in all this are the increasingly dominant forms of what Rob Nixon has described as "slow violence" and the temporalities peculiar to them: "Violence is customarily conceived as an event or action that is immediate in time, explosive and spectacular in space, and as erupting into instant sensation visibility. We need, I believe, to engage a different kind of violence, a violence that is neither spectacular nor instantaneous, but rather incremental and accretive, its calamitous repercussions playing out across a range of temporal scales."[1]

A transition in political thought and action away from intragenerational narcissism and toward an intergenerational perspective would require extensive, species-wide training in the logics of exponential developments, a crash course in matters of slow violence, and a geopolitics capable of finding its way out of its fixation on the present and toward post-contemporary decision criteria.

"Politics today," writes Daniel Falb, "can only mean geopolitics."[2] And as always when the political in an emphatic sense is concerned – i.e. in dealing with new, previously unheard-of and invisible political subjects such as the refugee – here, too, what is at issue is the integration of new subjects into the realm of politics. Not only the climate, animals, oceans, and other non-human agents like intelligent machines should be an active part of the political debate, but also subjects who do not even exist yet: our descendants.

THE FUTURE ISN'T WHAT IT USED TO BE – Language, grammar, and in particular a sophisticated tense system allow us to express and understand complex temporal relationships. To understand, for example, why it is by no means contradictory to think of the past – from the perspective of an even more remote past – as being in the future, or the future as soon to be in the past.

The past was once the future, the future will become the past, and we as human beings are accustomed to locating ourselves in the present. At the same time, however, we are always already beyond this present. Heidegger spoke in this respect of an *ecstatic temporality of Dasein*, with "Da-Sein" (literally, "being there") here denoting a specific spatial and above all temporal disposition. No one is ever simply here and now. The present is asynchronous; we are constantly moving beyond it. This ec-static dimension is today being explored technologically in complex societies in which we, together with machines, no longer exist in a singular present.

SITUATIVE THOUGHT AND TEMPORAL CATEGORIES – In his efforts to formulate a no longer dogmatic, but critical metaphysics, the analytical philosopher Sebastian Rödl draws on a conception of time as "the form of a sensory intuition through which thought has an object" and of "the general form of thought" as "the unity of thought whose object is given in intuition."[3] Against any (anti-)metaphysical skepticism that distinguishes between thought and intuition or is suspicious of any connection between them as baseless metaphysical speculation, Rödl understands reference to truth and consciousness of time as two sides of the same cognitive form. Intuition-dependent thought relates to that which exists in time, just as "time is the form of intuition that provides thought with an object."[4]

Following a long and problematic metaphysical tradition, Rödl situates human thought and behavior between animal and divine thought and behavior, but he does so via an original argument concerning the structure of grammatical tense. Human thought is situational, while the behavior of animals is always situation-responsive and timeless. "Presence" acquires a temporal meaning only for human beings, and only because we make temporally situated statements in language are we able to formulate statements that are timelessly true beyond the present. Even a divine intellect ultimately has no consciousness of time: "What an animal perceives is below time, what the divine intellect intuits is above time. [...] Time-consciousness is the unity of sensibility and understanding that defines man."[5]

As opposed to a tense-logical intellect, which according to Rödl relates only to the content of tense-logical formulae, from which it cannot free itself, human beings think in terms of their (fundamentally asynchronous) present. But this situational extemporality made possible not least by grammatical tenses – the shifting of language into the past or future tense, which brings us out of the present and into a different position – does not actually free us from every form of tense logic. As linguists from Gustave Guillaume to Elisabeth Leiss have shown, our grammar also requires an operative time, the *chronogenesis* of a certain time or temporal logic. The temporal model of past, present, and future chronogenetically produced by our tense system is a chrono-logical model. Our species, too, has at its disposal a tense logic called chronology.

LIVING IN A TIME COMPLEX – The impression that *times change* is ubiquitous, although "time" itself here is for the most part "thought" as a quasi-neutral container for events or social conditions that change "in it." This often flippantly tossed-off cliché is one that merits being taken seriously, particularly in the twenty-first century. Rather than asserting that changes take place in time, and then reflexively lamenting their accelerated pace, it might be helpful instead to warm up to the idea that we are in fact living in a different time. What if time itself has changed?

We are accustomed to orienting ourselves by a concept of linear time. The basic chrono-logical assumption is that time originates in the past and runs – hopefully, and always bringing with it new events – through the present in the direction of the future. It is just as plausible or even more plausible, however, to assume that in complex societies, time instead moves backward from the future. Complex social formations such as our own are distinguished by technological infrastructures increasingly characterized by automation, robotization, and algorithmization. The accompanying loss of human primacy is associated with a loosening or loss of our anchoring in the present.

Even at a purely biological level, our thoughts, perceptions, and feelings initially anchor us in a present out of which we then act, a present that in complex technological infrastructures has ever less power to assert itself. The hypothesis of a fundamental change in time is thus that we are living in a new time, a new technological time complex.

THE A-T-M COMPLEX OR THE EVOLUTION OF TIME – Empirical evidence from various fields of linguistics is now converging on a theory of the relational development of grammatical categories, i.e. that the category of aspect (A) develops first, then the category of tense (T), and finally mood or modality (M). Grammatical categories thus emerge and evolve and accordingly can also "age." In terms of the history of language, then, the category of aspect develops into the category of tense, which further evolves into the category of mood (e.g. the imperfective aspect evolves into the imperfect past tense, from which then proceed the irrealis moods).

The theory of an A-T-M complex in no way implies that languages with highly developed tense systems have attained a higher evolutionary status than those which possess only aspect, or that the subjunctive mood allows us to express modalities which speakers of other languages simply do not have at their disposal. Both temporal and modal relations can be apprehended and communicated in language using already available grammatical structures. The lesson of the complex relation of aspect, tense, and mood is rather that tenses also possess an aspectual dimension, and that moods evolve from tenses, as can be seen from similarities between the future tense and the subjunctive mood (will/would, shall/should).

All moods are temporal and cannot even be thought of as atemporal. Only tense can establish mood, not vice versa. Like mood, possibility, virtuality, and ultimately change are all based in time, for which reason a narrowing of time or of our understanding of time also means reducing our possibilities for action. Not only what is new, but even time itself, cannot be reduced to the actualization of what has already been laid out in the past. Rather, time allows a virtuality to emerge that did not already exist in (past) time. We must understand tense in terms of modality. We must again conceive of the future as contingent (rather than as predetermined).

IS THE PAST TRULY PAST, ONCE AND FOR ALL? – During the discussion following a lecture, the moderator expresses his apprehension that certain phenomena, which he and other progressive thinkers considered to be bygone, are once again becoming current. "We thought that was in the past," he says – by which he means that he hopes these phenomena *are* in the past.

From a leftist or progressive perspective, but now articulated more technically and precisely in terms of grammatical tense, the danger and the new insight today is that the past used to be past, or at least seemed to have been past. We would like past events to remain in the past, i.e. we would like the past to *be* past – this is what we thought up until quite recently. Instead, we see today that the past *was* past, but that unfortunately it *is* once again current. And it is even to be feared that this past could become, will be, or is the future.

THE ANCESTRAL PAST – Quentin Meillassoux offers a fascinating speculation about an absolute past completely divorced not just from our own thought, but from human time overall. The idea of what he calls the *ancestral* past came to him in light of fossils finds that according to geodetic calculations are several billion years old, i.e. that existed long before any perceiving entity, let alone any thinking entity – *arche-fossils*, which, in contrast to the overwhelming number of objects we encounter, existed without any correlation to a subject. (By way of contrast, Meillassoux designates all prior philosophy as correlationist, i.e. capable of conceiving of objects only in relation to subjects.) Nevertheless, thanks to rates of radioactive decay and to Meillassoux's speculative rethinking of these physical hypotheses, we now know about this past, which for us never was, never is or has been, and never will be. We thus know about a past that, in contrast to our subjective or objective human past (if such a thing is ever supposed to have existed), is never present for us, nor has it ever been present even to itself.

But with what justification are we then able to speak of an *original* past at all? The ancestral past is only a past for us, i.e. one that has been reconstituted for us by us. In and of itself, ancestrality is neither past nor present, present neither in nor for itself nor for anyone else. This speculation nevertheless fascinates us and says something about the asynchronous present in which we live, as well as about the future connected with it.

WHY WE WILL NEVER HAVE SEEN THE FUTURE — Almost three decades ago, Bruno Latour wrote a book with the title *We Have Never Been Modern*. More recently, he has added to this assessment a further surprising observation: "Contrary to what is often said about them, the Moderns are creatures who look not *forward* but almost exclusively *backward* and, curiously, *up in the air*. [...] Since they don't have eyes in the back of their heads, they completely *deny* [what] is coming toward them, as if they were too busy fleeing the horrors of the old days. Their vision of the future would seem to have blinded them to the direction in which they are headed; or, rather, it is as though what they mean by 'future' were entirely constituted by the rejection of their past, without any realistic content attached to the 'things to come.'"[6]

This assessment stands at odds with our temporal conception of ourselves, and not only as Moderns. From childhood, we learn to look from the present into the future, or to look away from the present in the service of a (better) future, i.e. we learn to make compromises, sacrificing the here and now to a future present. The shift from a pleasure principle to a reality principle as diagnosed by Freud means nothing other than mastering this concept of temporal deferral together with the winking implication that the bourgeois reality principle is the only reliable principle for affording pleasure. Even empiricists less inclined toward *metapsychology* (as Freud dubbed his own speculative excursions) acknowledge the so-called "marshmallow test" – in which children who resist immediately eating a marshmallow placed in front of them are rewarded with a promised second marshmallow – as demonstrating that the arduously phylo- and ontogenetically acquired ability to defer gratification makes us higher cognitive beings. As Michio Kaku explains, "[B]eing able to defer gratification also refers to a higher level of awareness and consciousness. These children were able to simulate the future and realize that future rewards were greater. So being able to see the future consequences of our actions requires a higher level of awareness."[7] Mutually accounting for both present and future thus seems to be a distinguishing characteristic not only of particular individuals, but of our species as a whole. And despite this, the charge is that we Moderns do not look into the future?

GOOGLE NOW TOMORROW – *Time is money*, goes the motto of money-minded modernity. Just-in-time production and delivery represent the dream of an industrial modernity that reacts immediately and exclusively to demand. Where the production of objects or goods is no longer concerned, as in the speculative finance industry, high-frequency traders spend billions for minimal time advantages, an edge of a few milliseconds made possible by high-speed fiberglass cable connections. And has not the company that epitomizes the new digital economy cemented this fixation on ever shorter presents in the very title of one of its most advanced applications, Google Now (the functionalities of which have since been integrated into the broader Google app)?

With its AdSense program and accompanying algorithm, Google has achieved what Ed Finn aptly refers to as "commoditizing the contemporary." The aim is to present us with the most precise and promising possible ads in our here and now using data obtained from us in the past (interests, preferences, locations, etc.). Standing behind this focus on the now, however, is no longer the present, but the very near future, a perverted version of what J. G. Ballard once promoted as *science fiction for the next five minutes.* Google Now "promises to organize not just the present but the near future temporalities of its users. It will suggest when to leave for the next meeting, factoring in traffic, creating an intimate, personal reminder system arbitraging public and private data."[8]

If we follow the title of Finn's book and ask "what algorithms want," the answer is nothing other than what Google assumes to be our secret desire, namely to help us finally be able to not have to constantly decide about the present here and now. Algorithms have since "cross[ed] the threshold from prediction to determination, from modeling to building cultural structures."[9]

It is only a small step from prediction to restriction. Or in the words of Google Now (and ever?): "The right information at just the right time. See information that you need throughout your day, before you even ask."

DERIVATIVE SUPREMACY AND OVERPOWERING THE FUTURE – It would seem as though the future – more specifically: a new model of the future – has finally overpowered the present. We see clear signs of this in the financial world, in macroeconomic decision-making processes at the national and international level as well as at the level of global financial markets.

One impressive example of this is the various financial rating agencies, whose power can scarcely be overstated. They assess not only private companies, but also the banks that finance them and even entire nations and national economies (although no one rates these non-transparent, undemocratic, and – as became clear during the most recent financial crisis – corrupt agencies themselves). Positive evaluations of the future development of a company or the future prospects of an economic sector or national economy *de facto* have massive effects on reality – effects that are quasi-retroactive in that they are projected from the future back onto the present. Indeed, what is more, negative assessments increase the cost of investment capital and as a direct result serve as confirmation of these very negative assessments, which thereby see themselves confirmed in their "scientificity."

We also encounter this sort of retroactive performance in the trading of derivatives, which Elie Ayache has dubbed the "technology of the future." The volume of outstanding derivative contracts on the various stock markets alone now exceeds that of the "real" economy many times over. The true significance of derivatives, however, consists in their chronogenetic power, their ability to establish a form of non-chronological time by making future possibilities tradeable and negotiable in the present. Regardless of which future present comes to pass, derivative transactions always derive their truth from the present future (i.e. the future assumed in the present). Simply put: today's assumptions about tomorrow overpower both the future and the present, as assumptions about the setting of prices automatically become true with every closing of a derivative contract.

The performative force of such contracts rests on a precarious form of non-reciprocity. What is generally presupposed in the case of a normal contract, namely that both parties are required to abide by it, is precisely not the case when it comes to speculative financial bets. At their core, the types of derivative contracts responsible for the last financial crisis (credit swaps, etc.) demolish this contractual logic. As Arjun Appadurai writes, "Looked at from the point of view that sees derivative contracts as a type of promise (performative in form), the credit default swap is actually a speculative bet on the certainty that one of the two parties who made a promise will break the promise."[10] No wonder, then, that not everything runs smoothly with the derivative management of the present from the future, this forced identification of present future and future present.

PREDICTION – PREVENTION – PREEMPTION – It is high time to distinguish historic forms of control (i.e. efforts to control the future) from those that we encounter in the present and from the future. The question can be rendered in grammatical terms as the alternative between understanding "control of the future" as a *subjective genitive* or as an *objective genitive* phrase, that is: whether we will control the future or whether the future will control us.

From the past, we are familiar with the concept of *prediction* as prophesying what will happen, i.e. a basically neutral view from the present concerning a future that must be adapted to. *Prevention* is more clearly determinate and at the same time more negative. Here a negative assessment and the will to avert what is to come go hand in hand. If we fear bad things will happen in the future, then we must change them or not allow them to occur in the first place.

Preemption – which is precisely the opposite of preventive avoidance of a negative prophecy, although the two are often confused – follows yet another temporal logic. This small, largely overlooked difference can be seen with respect to the most well-known form of the preemptive, and the first to emerge into general consciousness. The *preemptive warfare* waged and first elevated to a state of ab-normality by the George W. Bush administration, contrary to the official rhetoric of prevention, has led not to peace, but rather precisely to the prophesied situation that it promised to prophylactically avoid. Or, to modify a quote from Karl Kraus on psychoanalysis: The "war on terror" is the political illness for which it regards itself as a cure.

FROM PREVENTIVE VIOLENCE TO PREEMPTIVE POLICING – Countless attempts have been made to define the origin of the first state or political community. One explanation stands out, however: namely, that political structures originally emerged at the moment when it first seemed reasonable to transfer the exercise and thus the containment of violence to overriding institutions. With respect to modernity, this means that the state possesses a monopoly on violence. It alone may exercise violence, and precisely this is supposed to allow it (and the society pacified by it) generally to prevent or, in functioning societies, even potentially eliminate the occurrence of violence. This state monopoly on violence conforms to a temporal model of prevention, and a separation of the entities predestined to exercise violence – the police domestically, the military abroad – is also characteristic of democratic orders. The reduction of violence and ultimately the separation of powers in democracies is thus supposed to rest not on police deterrence, but on a model of prevention.

The preemptive and drone wars of recent years threaten the separation of powers into executive, legislative, and judicial branches constitutive of democratic societies. Multiple shifts have upset the naturally delicate balance of the ever-fragile structure of divided but mutually co-operating constitutional systems. To begin with, in preemptive drone strikes – which generally are initially "justified" in moral terms and at best given provisional legal justification only after the fact – the targets are always already guilty and condemned to death (a bit reminiscent of medieval witch tests). We are dealing here not with a political logic, but with a more or less unbounded police logic that neither abides nor must abide by judicial restrictions, nor does it limit itself to its original remit (i.e. the scope of the duties intended for it within the logic of a monopoly on violence).

There is a second transgression and diffusion of boundaries even more threatening than the increasing logistical and technological militarization of the police (the at times grotesque deployment, particularly in the United States, of abundantly available weaponry from an ever-growing number of military campaigns). We are contemporary witnesses to a gradual "policialization" of politics in strict accordance with the politically disastrous temporal logic of prevention. As Grégoire Chamayou writes, military organizations are now being tasked with "the sort of missions that normally are assigned to the police within a domestic framework: namely, the identification, tracking, location, and capture (but in actual fact the physical elimination) of suspect individuals,"[11] in what might be called a transnationalization of policing: "Whereas counterinsurgency is essentially politico-military, antiterrorism fundamentally has to do with policing and security."[12]

ALTERNATIVE PREHENSION – We owe our reflections on the concept of prehension, which also offers a political alternative to the current tendency to "preemptively" predetermine both the future and the present, to Alfred North Whitehead, one of the forefathers of contemporary speculative philosophy. In everyday language, "prehension" denotes the act of grasping. For Whitehead, it further expresses how entities generally behave toward each other and how inflowing information is received as well as transformed. Luciana Parisi points to this in her book *Contagious Architecture*, where she applies Whitehead's concept to the realm of computation: "[A]s actual occasions, algorithms prehend the formal system into which they are scripted, and also the external data inputs that they retrieve. Nevertheless, this activity of prehension does not simply amount to a reproduction of what is prehended. On the contrary, it can be described as a contagion.

This is because to prehend data is to undergo an irreversible transformation defined by the way in which rules are immanent to the infinite varieties of quantities that they attempt to synthesize. This means that rules cannot change these infinite quantities; instead the latter can determine rules anew and thus produce new ones."[13] We are dealing here with what in Parisi's speculative terminology may be called a *mereological* change in dominance – considering her polemic against parametric architecture, we can also speak here of "mereotopology" – when the parts become greater or more important than "their" whole, when a quantitative increase in data and parameters leads to a qualitative change: the dominance of data over its programming.

This speculative hypothesis aims at nothing less than a reversal of the usual relation between active program and passive data, the assumption that the former regulates or determines the latter. What if data (abductively) transform "their" algorithm, rather than being controlled by it (as in the case of deductive preemption)? Computation so understood would then be not a reflexive, but a recursive process, and we would be dealing not with a critical or reflexive procedure, but with "an example of a speculative reason that is concerned not with using numbers to predict the future, but with following algorithmic prehensions to decide the present. Algorithmic architecture is therefore but one example of the way in which this computation builds the present through the prehension of infinite data. Algorithmic architecture is thus a case of speculative computing exposing reason, logic, and calculation to the power of the incomputable."[14]

At the intersection of universal axioms and unpredictable data, prehension evokes a new temporality, and the unpredictability it introduces also reopens the horizon of the future, which prevention, prediction, and preemption all circumscribe in different ways or even cause to vanish entirely. A progressive approach to the new time complex could subsequently be linked to the question of whether what is foreign and other – and what else would a future worth its name be? – can be successfully integrated into its own present logic. Also progressive, in the literal sense of the word, would be an expansion of time (coming back from the future) in the direction of the past. *Le passé est imprévisible*, as Meillassoux once wrote: the past is unpredictable and just as original as the present. Time – a time – is progressive only when it allows richer, more numerous, and more contingent origins.

THE SPECTER OF HYPERSTITION – We are looking for ideas that will help us not only conceptualize, but also navigate the logic of cultural and political developments within the global network of capitalism. One candidate is the concept of *hyperstition*, a portmanteau of "hype" and "superstition," a term for fictions that realize themselves from the future.

Hyperstitions place the origins of our present in the future, raising the question of whether there can be a progressive approach to this new temporality and what this would look like. First and foremost, we must distinguish between right-wing and left-wing, fear-mongering/reactionary and progressive/emancipatory hyperstitions, which have long been among the techniques employed by minority populations who never cease to orient themselves by a possible different and better future. Examples of this include progressive ethnofuturisms, Gulf Futurism, Sino- or Shanghai Futurism, and especially the various Afrofuturistic waves in music, art, and pop culture over recent decades. Thus spoke Sun Ra: *The light of the future casts the shadows of tomorrow … The possible has been tried and failed. Now it's time to try the impossible.*

Truth

ALTERNATIVE THINKING – We are accustomed to equating thought and reflection, as though there were no alternative to our culturally injected reflexive thinking. Such reflexive and thus mirror-like thought constantly strives – whether implicitly or explicitly, consciously or unconsciously – to locate itself in the present of its object (and objective) counterpart. In truth, this process naturally always plays out retroactively, as a re-action.

Thinking the new, by contrast, always follows a recursive pattern. In recursive processes in which parts combine together to form new wholes, both integrating whole and integrated parts are changed, and this changing of the object of knowledge – which does not exist prior to, nor does it proceed in sync with cognition – necessarily also induces a transformation of the discerning (or researching, artistic) subject. This applies as well to thought about or from the future that is conscious of this recursivity and seeks to exploit or even enhance it. We are dealing here with a form of speculative thought, less reflexive than recursive, that is constantly assembling new elements and parts into a different whole. In place of the respective object of external and re-flexive thought, this requires – not least for political reasons – involved, participatory, recursive thinking.

WHAT HOLDS THE WORLD TOGETHER AT ITS CORE: A PANORAMA – Recursion, according to linguists, stands as the sole remaining candidate for a universal element belonging to all languages. Morphologically (*go—going—gone*) as well as semantically (*go under—undergo*) and above all syntactically (*We must—We must be going—We must be going crazy*), an infinite quantity of meaning can be generated from a limited pool of sounds, words, and rules by continuously adding new parts that change the meaning both of what came before and of what is added, producing with every word, every clause or parenthetical, a new a whole and therefore a new meaning, ad infinitum, without ever coming or having to come to an end ... Recursion is thus that universal operator which adds parts to a constantly changing whole and generates new meaning.

Recursion as modified selectivity occurs not only at the level of highly developed languages, but even at the fundamental level of our biology. As Terrence W. Deacon writes in his book *Incomplete Nature: How Mind Emerged from Matter*, "Organisms are not built or assembled; they grow by the multiplication of cells, a process of division and differentiation from prior, less differentiated precursors. Both in development and in phylogeny, wholes precede parts, integration is intrinsic, and design occurs spontaneously. The machine metaphor is a misleading oversimplification."[15]

This difference from machines can also be seen at another level of recursive operations, namely, in our brains, whose neural networks differ from processor architectures in that complex bundles of neurons are constantly relinking themselves in new ways to create new neural pathways. In the words of the theoretical physicist and string theorist Michio Kaku: "Neural networks have a completely different architecture from that of digital computers. If you remove a single transistor in the digital computer's central processor, the computer will fail. However, if you remove large chunks of the human brain, it can still function, with other parts taking over for the missing pieces."[16] Here again we see the flexibility of recursive structures, which is ultimately also responsible for our self, that "recursive information integration system," as R. Scott Bakker calls it, whose "peculiar structural characteristics we associate with the first-person perspective."[17]

No wonder, then, that in addition to our biology and our brain, social structures are also constructed according to a recursive pattern. As James Trafford explains, "Interactions give rise to norms when the relevant interactional activities reinforce certain patterns of behavior as acceptable, or unacceptable, in social practices through recursively acting upon those underlying patterns. This can be understood in terms of recursive feedback loops that are generated through the interactions between patterns of behavior, and so are apiece with the mechanisms that also generate patterns of behavior, through mechanisms of differential response."[18]

Finally, recursive relations between part and whole also make possible life on earth, as well as a holistic planetary context that James Lovelock somewhat misleadingly calls *Gaia*. "Evolution in the context of Gaia brings in the material environment in a way that is absent from Darwinian evolution. Quite simply, if the evolution of an organism changes the material environment in a way that affects further evolution, then the two processes become tightly coupled."[19] Our planet is not simply a mass of predominantly liquid rock that just so happens to be surrounded by a well-tempered crust, some water, and air. Rather, life has always been an integral coherence of constant recursive influences, (co-)responsible for the amount of CO_2 in the atmosphere and the salt content of the oceans.

Hence in place of a constricted theory of evolution, Lovelock, Latour, and Donna Haraway – who argues that "[i]f it is true that neither biology nor philosophy any longer supports the notion of independent organisms in environments, that is, interacting units plus contexts/ rules, then sympoiesis is the name of the game in spades"[20] – all recommend that not just natural scientists but society as a whole convert to a less autopoietic than *sympoietic* or *symbiogenetic* Darwinism, the basic operators of which are not one-sided, reactive responses of species to their environment, but rather mutual recursive adaptations of categories such as "life" and "environment" (which are always and everywhere *differentiable*, even if they cannot be conceived apart from one another).

The interactive (and transgenerational) dynamic whereby organisms influence their environment (termite mounds, beehives, etc.) is also known as ecological niche construction. As Gary Tomlinson writes, "Niche construction is not restricted to the evolution of hominins, of course, but instead is ubiquitous in the history of life. Its fundamental systemic pathway is a *feedback circuit*," the mutual evolutionary influencing of organisms and ecosystems. In addition to such feedback loops, Tomlinson also refers to "control mechanisms directing niche constructive cycles from the outside. Such external controls are not feedback at all, whether positive or negative; instead they are *feedforward* elements. Feedforward had always been important in niche construction: climatic variations, geological changes ranging from volcanism to tectonic plate movements, and astronomical cycles are all feedforward elements in relation to the niche construction of earthly organisms."[21]

What this brief panorama shows is that recursion occurs at every level. From our cells to the atmosphere, from our individual thought processes to our social structures, recursion regulates and governs as a universal operator. If we continue not to understand this, if we fail to understand that we cannot understand our existence and our world purely *reflexively*, we will pay a corresponding price. Any progressive intellectual (metaphysical) or social and (eco-) political solution will have to be one which has comprehended and learned how to deal with the recursive structure of our universe.

IN THE BEGINNING WAS THE SENTENCE – In the beginning, according to the New Testament, was *logos*. The truth expressed here refers not to a single word, however, but a sentence, a linguistic structure that generates meaning out of the difference of its components.

The ability to calibrate and understand

differential components requires corresponding cognitive faculties that naturally evolve not subsequent to, but in parallel with our linguistic and other cultural developments. R. Scott Bakker's hypothesis that "[a]t some point in our recent evolutionary past, perhaps coeval with the development of language, the human brain became more and more *recursive*, which is to say, more and more able to factor its own processes into its environmental interventions,"[22] must be defined more precisely in this sense, as our brain has always developed in parallel with our capacity for language.

Terrence Deacon's theory of the *co-evolution of language and the brain* also offers the possibility of giving more evolutionary nuance to Noam Chomsky's theory of an inborn capacity for language or original language instinct: "Languages have adapted to human brains and human brains have adapted to languages, but the rate of language change is hundreds or thousands of times more rapid than biological change. [...] The brain has co-evolved with respect to language, but languages have done most of the adapting."[23] Language and thought, language and reality form a recursively ordered coherence. Reality, (its) meaning, and linguistic material (sounds, written words, etc.) are not simply arbitrarily (un)related to each other; in the beginning was communication through the structure of language. A lexical system conveys referents with signifieds; grammar, signifiers with signifieds. Language situates us in the world – inscribes us in the world – and helps us change it. You, he, here, there, yesterday, tomorrow: only through the constant calibration of such expressions (called "deictic shifters"), which are empty in and of themselves, do we arrive at concrete views of ourselves and others.

Language is therefore not – as many armchair philosophers and philosophers of language believe – that which separates us from reality. For an ontology that is up to date on the state of twenty-first-century linguistic research, language and being are not mutually exclusive. Indeed, an ontological theory is inherent in the structure of language itself. The world that language communicates to us consists not of objects, but of relations and connections. And with its immanent knowledge of the nature of the world, language can claim a higher degree of realism than our perception, whose "sensuous certainty"

(Hegel) would only ever lose sight of me and you yesterday here and tomorrow there.

LANGUAGE MAGIC 2.0 – Notions about the magical power of language enjoy a long tradition – from Kabbalah and the Gospel of John (with the idea of an original divine naming of things that also takes into account the syntacticity of language) to Jacob Böhme's linguistic mysticism and Novalis' *Monologue* (with the idea of language as primarily communicating only with itself and thereby all the more with the world) to Walter Benjamin's linguistic-philosophical efforts to dissolve the *crusted surface* of things through *contact with a magnetic force*, with language here conceived not as a means to an end, but as establishing a connection to a spiritual or mental being: "It is fundamental that this mental being communicates itself *in* language and not *through* language."[24]

We find clear traces of this tradition today in the idea of our reality as a universal operating system – including paranoid fears that we are all part of preprogrammed matrix. At the center of this is the algorithm, "the object at the intersection of computational space, cultural systems, and human cognition." Hence, Ed Finn writes, "[w]e need a deeper understanding of the algorithm in order to understand how computational systems are transforming our world today. In that sense this is a literacy exercise, an experiment in developing an 'algorithmic reading' of the world."[25] In the twenty-first century, the world again appears as a book (though this time a digital one): a text or secret code in possession of a few monopolies that enjoy interpretational sovereignty, and only to be cracked by shamanic heretics, whom we now call hackers.

This hypothesis of a digital or programmed book of the world requires a double differentiation in terms of what distinguishes human language from other languages. First, with respect to biosemioticians who go as far as to extend the so-called semiosphere to microbes, plants, and our own DNA, we must insist on the distinction between informational and semiotic relations. As Gary Tomlinson writes, drawing on the semiotic theory developed by Charles Sanders Peirce, plants, microorganisms, and the like "are non-semiotic organisms, while most vertebrates, including amphibians, reptiles, mammals, and birds, are sign-makers. [...] This is not to deny that trees and paramecia and clams stand in hugely complex relation to their environments and the stimuli they receive from them. Theirs is not a semiotic relation, however, but an *informational* one, without interpretants or signs."[26]

Second, human language is to be distinguished from artificial languages. Particularly in the age of the internet as a hypertext constantly producing new feedback loops, we cannot ignore the fact that recursivity works differently in natural and in computer languages. This corresponds to a paradigm shift brought about by recent advances in algorithmic speech analysis made possible by immense quantities of data and computing power. "The major breakthroughs in algorithmic speech analysis have come by abandoning deep linguistic structure – efforts to thoroughly map grammar and semantics – in favor of treating speech as a statistical, probabilistic challenge."[27]

The more we abandon the hope that machines will actually be able to understand our language, the better they understand what we say. Communication between different linguistic or semiotic forms of recursion as well as reciprocal feedback loops between human beings and machines are then possible on this basis. (Siri adapts to dialects, users to the machine's ability to understand them.) Even as a digital book, the world contains many different languages, and above all: different logics of language.

FEEDFORWARD WITH RECURSION AND ABDUC-TION – "Deduction proves that something *must* be; Induction shows that something *actually is* operative; Abduction merely suggests that something *may be*," writes the founder of semiotics and inventor of the alternative logical procedure of abduction, Charles Sanders Peirce.[28]

Abductions are responsible for creating the new, hence their importance particularly in current AI research as well as wherever explanatory hypotheses are formulated. Rather than deriving the particular from the general or, conversely, a general rule from individual cases, abduction is a form of logical inference in which both an individual phenomenon and its conformity to natural laws are educed in parallel. This is applicable wherever conventional logical procedures are no longer effective, whether deductive reasoning that infers individual cases from already available rules or inductive reasoning that allows us to believe that we can derive universal laws from things we seem to have a firm empirical grasp on. In the third millennium, it is instead time for thought and action that not only do not suppress the constant shifting of object and rule, part and whole, but understand how to exploit their mutual influence on each other.

Only recursive, abductive, speculative thinking – "The speculative process described by Whitehead is roughly similar to what Charles Sanders Peirce calls abduction," writes Steven Shaviro[29] – is capable of finding solutions to those problems that we will encounter in the future and from the future. When questions and phenomena approach us from the future, we can no longer comprehend them, as metaphysical tradition or everyday understanding would have it, by assuming a correspondence between matter and mind (*adaequatio rei et intellectus*, reads the corresponding maxim attributed to Thomas Aquinas, the most important medieval Christian philosopher). Truth does not simply objectively exist in the present. Nor, however, is it merely subjective, as relativists of all eras have proclaimed. In actuality, truth emerges over time and must always first be constructed. Following Hegel, truth is not simply (the image of) reality, but the unity of possibility and reality in our understanding of the world. Only via a recursive imperative can subjunctive possibilities become indicative realities.

Reality

UNIVERSALISM – REALISM – NOMINALISM – It may well be that the whole history of philosophy, its recurring problems, schisms, and central trajectories, will ultimately be written as a history of grappling with the question of what can actually be understood as reality. Debates over realism, nominalism, and universalism – to name just a few relevant philosophical terms – make it possible to draw fundamental distinctions between different authors and schools, while at the same time elucidating the impossibility of ever arriving once and for all at a single philosophical conception of reality.

Such debates have been waged since the beginnings of Western philosophy. Even Aristotle departed from Plato, who posited the existence of forms independent of concrete things, universals and original attributes (such as "tableness" or "blueness") that according to Platonists exist not just *in rebus* (in objects) but *ante rebus* (prior to and independent of objects). At the other end of the realism debate, we find what is called nominalism, according to which there exist no universals but only particular individual things and generalizations based solely on the formation of rational concepts (via our naming of things, the use of nouns). This schism is repeated in modernity in debates on critical versus dogmatic philosophy (at the latest since Kant, whose three epochal critiques are not, as is often assumed, directed against metaphysics as such, but rather explore the possibility of a critical metaphysics).

The question of reality, of whether we should dedicate ourselves to trying to ascertain *what* things themselves are, or limit ourselves to the question of *whether* and *how* we are able to cognize them in the first place, stands at the center of the always impending divide between speculation and epistemology. This metaphysical schism, which also threatens to reduce the significance of metaphysics itself, looms and emerges in philosophy again and again. It is moreover a dual schism, as not only does philosophy itself (which is always metaphysical) hereby limit itself, but its retreat from things also does no good for the increasingly isolated subject of cognition as, at times, the sole remaining focus of philosophical attention.

As in the examples from antiquity mentioned above and at the turn of the nineteenth century, our concern today is finding solutions for a realistic metaphysics – or as Ray Brassier writes, "[T]he metaphysical exploration of the structure of being can only be carried out in tandem with an epistemological investigation into the nature of conception. For we cannot understand *what* is real unless we understand what 'what' *means*, and we cannot understand what 'what' means without understanding what 'means' *is*, but we cannot hope to understand what 'means' is without understanding what 'is' *means*. [...] For just as epistemology without metaphysics is empty, metaphysics without epistemology is blind."[30] What is required is thus a speculative metaphysics, i.e. one that thinks with eyes open to reality.

TWO DIAMETRICALLY OPPOSED REALISMS —
Historians, literary theorists, and scholars of
the arts have delineated an interesting shift in
the meaning of what in the nineteenth century
was described as "the real," which developed in
conjunction with a then-new literary and artistic
interest in highly different social realities. *Le
réel* now referred to opposing phenomena – the
beautiful as well as the ugly, good as well as evil,
the ideal as well as the positive – and increasingly also to grotesque elements. This expansion
of meaning was accompanied by a broadening
of the scope of the subject matter of realistic
narration. Realism and the real ran in parallel and were as a matter of course understood
to be part of reality. Depicting as many real
details as possible was further associated with the
will to change the social reality thus narrated or
described.

The twentieth century, meanwhile, was characterized by a diametrically opposed realism
of narration or of signifiers. Exponents of the
political and artistic avant-garde argued that
formalization and abstraction – procedures
purportedly opposed to realistic representation
– were in fact *more realistic*. The twentieth cen-

tury's *passion du réel* (Alain Badiou) consisted in finding, behind apparent occurrences, behind the screen, and behind the ideology of society, a different, truer reality which, it was consequently believed, one could only arrive at by means of a revolutionary effort directed against existing reality. Only within this model could one conceive of something like a *traumatic realism* (Hal Foster) or arrive at the idea that art – as part of what Lacan called the *symbolic* – serves as a protective shield against a real that is in and of itself unbearable (and as such also inaccessible).

No wonder that the dominance of this realism was and is haunted by a kind of constantly recurring symptom, a ceaselessly heralded "return" of realism or the real. It would be incorrect simply to ascribe this to a longing for times past. Rather, it is an indication that neither of the two logics, orders, or regimes of realism possesses a conclusive answer. What is more, it may be that today both realisms are past their prime.

A NEW REALISM OF REFERENCE? – The category of realism is once again being fiercely fought over, suggesting that there continue to be deep divisions separating our various conceptions of reality. Yet even positions that are staunchly opposed to one another nevertheless exhibit similarities that, if they do not permit any conclusive systematization, may at least serve as initial indicators of an understanding of reality and realism that is peculiar to the twenty-first century.

Behind the still incessantly proclaimed crises of reality and returns of realism – in the novel, in film, on television, and, combining and enhancing all of these, on platforms like Netflix – stands, first and foremost, a need for significance and meaning. (An example of this from the world of theater would be Milo Rau's interventions, in which the real is constantly made fictional and the fictional made real, i.e. in which reality and fiction are mutually made true, though without this resulting in any postmodern indifference to the distinction between reality and simulation.) Significance and meaning must first be produced through narrations and fictions, not simply by fictional means, but via recursive procedures. New connections are thereby established, forming a linked series that "*passes across* the difference between things and words." According to Bruno Latour, "reference" here designates "*the quality of the chain in its entirety*, and no longer *adaequatio rei et intellectus*."[31]

The problem or the starting point of such a referential realism is thus no longer human beings' designation of or reference to reality or the discovery of the real in or behind reality. Priority is rather given to the production of reality, of new meanings and connections between things, words, and people (without the latter necessarily taking on the exclusive role of positing said meanings). This raises the question of how stable connections can be constructed if the correlationist assumption that things ultimately obtain their meaning from us human beings is no longer self-evident. Reality in the twenty-first century neither depends on us (our attribution of significance or meaning), nor does it simply always already exist before our eyes, as a naive realism would have us believe. We must move beyond the dichotomy that either "the real" is simply available to us or we have only limited and relative access to "things."

Various speculative approaches in philosophy, such as the speculative realism or speculative materialism of Quentin Meillassoux, also serve as an indication of this forward-looking constellation of the real, reality, and realism. Meillassoux's "entire enterprise consists in maintaining that *we can without inconsistency think what there is when there is no thought*, thus being able to think a certain form of *absolute* [i.e. the real] that is non-relative to our mental categories."[32]

In this future regime, the real does not stand in opposition to reality, but nor does it simply exist before our eyes. Reality is conceivable, but we cannot conceive it without scientific or speculative effort. We have access to reality, but only by means of speculation. This goes against the view, heretofore dominant also in philosophy, that there is a correlation between mind and world, which led to a shift in focus away from things, the real, and reality, and toward our contact with them, i.e. ultimately toward ourselves.

Relativistic and correlationist philosophy has all too long sought to evade reality, instead devoting itself (anthropocentrically or narcissistically) to itself. This has led to an intellectual dead end and a crisis of reality. For this reason, too, we are in need of a new speculative and materialist philosophy. The realism of the future will have been a materialism.

THE REALITY OF INSTITUTIONS – Institutions regulate how we behave, and they do so by controlling our expectations. The fact that we always already know – or believe that we know, but this makes no difference – what conduct will be rewarded or sanctioned makes *institutionalization*, according to the sociologist M. Rainer Lepsius, "a process of mediation between 'culture' and 'society.'"[33] We increasingly encounter the accusation, however, that existing (cultural) institutions no longer observe their function in our society. Hence it is no wonder that such fossils, which reproduce nothing but antiquated content and values, are endowed with ever less government funding.

Rather than simply agreeing with such undifferentiated and unproductive criticism, however, we must take a closer look. Institutions unfortunately do largely lack the self-reflection necessary to comprehend their internal contradictions. For this reason alone, it is imperative to make use of the difference between what institutions purport to do or believe they do, and what they actually do. Indeed, grappling with the serious divergence between the actual effects of institutions and the intentions of their representatives can be highly productive. This concerns, for example, the ideological discrepancy – ideology here understood as a conglomerate of concepts and ideas that not so much relate to reality as obscure it – between the professed values and the everyday routines of our universities, or between the critical attitude that contemporary art claims to adopt and the real effects of the global art system.

What is needed is not a merely reflexive Institutional Critique (which has by now itself become institutionalized), but a recursive utilization of the real effects of institutions. Underlying this approach is the hypothesis that the influence of cultural institutions on society is far greater than these institutions for the most part assume. Only their real effects do not always lie where they are generally believed or hoped to lie. The institutions of contemporary art, for example, no differently than is to be expected of a flourishing worldwide enterprise, have immense local and global economic effects, which however are mostly either denied or acknowledged with a bad conscience, rather than being proactively (and productively) exploited. How do exhibiting institutions, for example, increase the value of art (without themselves profiting from it)? How do they influence market trends, and can they also influence geopolitical and ideological agendas?

Our educational institutions, particularly the humanities, likewise need to be reoriented away from their august content toward those real values and effects that they have always transported and produced through their institutional processes. Accordingly, an institutional realism is interested in the real, often profane or banal effects of institutions on society as a whole. Understanding how institutions operate socially and endeavoring to change them go hand in hand. Institutions are not the Other of the individuals who so love to complain about them and believe that they are hindered by their development.

Politics

A NEW POLITICAL SUBJECT WITHOUT A NEW
POLITICS – Are human beings by their nature
rational animals, an *animal rationale*? Or is man
even more originally a *zoon politicon*, a political animal, as Aristotle argues against an entire
phalanx of modern, neoclassical, and neoliberal
authors – beginning with Hobbes, Locke, and
Rousseau – who imagined a rational individual
striving for his or her own advantage at (or before)
the beginning of every social union? According to
these writers, politics is but a necessary evil in the
interest of all for the purpose of managing violence
between individuals. Among its corresponding
institutions are various cornerstones (or fetishes?)
of modern liberal democracies (and theorists of

democracy like Francis Fukuyama), including accountable governments and an independent judiciary, which constitute statehood.

If we consider the political economy of recent decades, however, we see that at least three of the pillars of a stable political and economic order find themselves in a massive crisis. More and more, in an age of globalization, the notions of fixed national borders and state sovereignty can be maintained only with violence. Confidence in the productivity of a manageable populace is vanishing in the face of growing surplus populations and ever larger migration flows. And since the last financial crisis, faith in a stable, self-organizing economic sphere free of all government or other forms of control is scarcely to be found even among fierce proponents of the free market economy. It is debatable whether we possess the means to counter in any way the pathologies, extreme conditions, and (seeming) anomalies that characterize modern politics and the modern economy – growing inequality, increasing corruption, reduced profit margins, and the stagnation of entire real economies – let alone whether we are capable of enacting measures such as massive redistribution or worldwide debt relief.

Marx once saw in the proletariat a revolutionary subject. In the geopolitical and economic constellations of the present, a new political subject is discernable in the form of the refugee. In the wretched no longer only of the earth, but of the sea, is manifested the inexcludability of the excluded, as well as the need for a genuine politicization of postcolonial capitalist globalization. Instead of viewing the refugee solely as a problematic figure, the task of a progressive politics today and tomorrow is instead to mobilize the refugee as a productive concept. The vanishing point of such a politics is what Daniel Falb calls a *planetarische Freizügigkeit*, a universal freedom of movement and generosity of spirit culminating in global citizenship for all.

REFUGEE POLICY VS. POLITICS OF THE REFUGEE – If we believe contemporary reporting and commentary on political events, political and economic crises are growing worse and worse and recurring in ever faster cycles. The resulting armed conflicts produce ever larger migration flows in which, along with economic and political refugees, the number of climate refugees will soon dramatically increase.

For this reason, refugees are precisely not the anomalies that politicians and populations who are stuck in the past so desperately want to see them as. Refugees are *the* new political subject of the twenty-first century, who now permit themselves – like their predecessors in the nineteenth and twentieth centuries: the bourgeoisie, women, workers, and then non-white ethnicities – to abandon their no-longer-bearable traditional place, to emerge onto the political stage, to speak, to be heard in unheard-of ways, and to create unrest in the *polis*.

The *barbaric* refugee (barbaric in the original sense of the word, i.e. not having mastered or refusing to speak the language of the ruling people) is evidently a lone objection against what is commonly understood as politics – namely, "the aggregation and consent of collectivities [...], the organization of powers, the distribution of places and roles, and the systems for legitimizing this distribution"[34] – but which according to the political philosopher Jacques Rancière ought instead to be called policing: "I now propose to reserve the term *politics* for an extremely determined activity antagonistic to policing [...]. Political activity is whatever shifts a body from the place assigned to it or changes a place's destination. It makes visible what had no business being seen, and makes heard a discourse where once there was only place for noise."[35]

The subjectivization of refugees is a de-identifying one, not only for the refugees themselves, who must break away from their old order, but also for every society with which they come in contact. With this newcomer in the political sphere, who previously was neither seen nor heard – at the least, it seems that profiteers have managed to be blind to colonialism and other forms of exploitation – and whose emergence does not come without resistance, the old economic and political order is beginning to unravel. At the same time, the refugee is an indicator of a new post-Anthropocene or post-Capitalocene politics which the established powers that be can naturally see only as illegitimate disorder.

The resulting refugee policies (which include halfhearted policies of integration) are the exact opposite of a modern politics of the refugee. Spatial questions about where refugees come from and where they should go potentially overlook their critical temporal dimension. What if the refugee's line of flight is toward the future?

THE NEW POLITICAL LAWS OF THE POST-ANTHROPOCENE – Ever since the time of Moses, we think of laws as being etched in stone, or at least grounded in the earth (*nomos* being the Greek term for both law and the division of land). This is changing in an age of rapid climate change, which is also producing geological and geopolitical abnormalities and, with the foreseeable changes to coastlines that in principle have been stable for millennia, calling into question the territorial primacy of political theory (i.e. the always presupposed natural primacy of the land over the sea).

With a view to the past, the jurist Davor Vidas writes: "The main development of the law of the sea, initiated in the aftermath of World War II, drew on a geological basis: viewing the continental shelf as a submarine prolongation of the land territory of coastal states. The key argument here was that mineral (fossil) resources of that submarine area belong geologically to the same pool as those resources found on the land which forms part of the same continental mass."[36] This is changing under the conditions of the Anthropocene, as the sea – increasingly and not coincidentally *the* zone to which refugees are fated – threatens to dominate and overwhelm the land. "In practice we are already in the Anthropocene (regardless of formal confirmation) – and the problem that will increasingly confront us is that international law, as codified today, is still based on the implicit assumption of enduring Holocene conditions."[37]

This discrepancy demonstrates that in (geo) political terms, we no longer find ourselves on the "terrain" of the twentieth century. Politically, too, we are witnesses of a historical intersection, at the necessary origin of a new techno-anthropo-capitalocene politics of the future.

MEREOTOPOLITICS OR SUBLIMATION OF POLITICS: EARTH – WATER – AIR – Even after the end of the Second World War, the legal scholar and political philosopher Carl Schmitt justified his defense of Nazi Germany's territorial logic vis-à-vis sea powers like England – the new air power of the United States played only a minor role, and only in his later years did he demonstrate any sensitivity for the "waves of space" – with recourse to the original primacy of the *nomos of the earth*, which today is met with ever greater competition thanks to advances in military and climate technology.

The new *nomoi* are (too) fluid and airy, and accordingly we observe desperate efforts to politically and juridically limit the effects of technological change. In his book *A Theory of the Drone*, Grégoire Chamayou describes how "a whole contingent of U.S. lawyers today claim that the notion of a 'zone of armed conflict' should no longer be interpreted in a strictly geographic sense. That geocentric concept, supposedly out of date, is now opposed to a target-centered one that is attached to the bodies of the enemy-prey."[38] Even in purely territorial disputes, the old geographical and geopolitical logic no longer holds, but shifts depending on where the protagonists are located at the moment. "To put that in very schematic terms, we have switched from the horizontal to the vertical, from the two-dimensional space of the old maps of army staffs to geopolitics based on volumes."[39]

Without doubt, we are dealing here with one of the central problems of future political metaphysics, in which nothing less than the nature of politics itself is at stake. "[The] debate over the respective merits of ground and air warfare," Chamayou writes, "is of a quasi-metaphysical nature: can counterinsurgency rise to the level of an aero-policy without losing its soul? There is of course a risk that in the course of the operation, the strategy – together with politics – may be lost in the clouds."[40] The old criteria and divisions of territorial contention are evaporating in the light of a spatial order that is no longer two- but multi-dimensional and a liquefaction of the territorial resulting from climate change. The new political (re)configuration of earth, water, and air is still awaiting a corresponding mereological politics that will bring together these individual elements to form a new whole, a new mereopolitics or mereotopolitics.

NEW MILITARY ETHICS AND MILITARY-METAPHYSICAL DIS/ORDER – Grégoire Chamayou does not simply analyze a new technological component of war, but develops the rudiments of a new political philosophy. The deployment of robots and drones is exemplary of a post-democratic syndrome that feels compelled to justify itself to its own populace (the promise of security, cost pressures) while at the same time insisting on the sovereignty of nation states with their unbroken will to wage war.

We are confronted here with questions of political theory and moral philosophy similar to those now being debated, in a much more innocuous form, in the context of self-driving cars – who decides in the case of an unavoidable accident, whose life should be spared, whose death taken into account, etc. Robots also promise fewer accidents, as they are able to kill more rationally. At the same time, war crimes committed by killing machines raise corresponding political *and* metaphysical questions: Is the robot at fault, its programmer, or the strategy of the commanding general? The drones increasingly deployed in recent years have only deepened the problem. "This weapon extends and radicalizes the existing processes of remote warfare and ends up by doing away with combat. But in so doing, it is the very notion of 'war' that enters into crisis. A central problem arises: if the 'war of drones' is no longer quite warfare, what kind of 'state of violence' does it amount to?"[41] Not unlike Socrates, who once approached military representatives in the agora of Athens in order to ask them (as men who all certainly waged only just wars) loaded questions about justice as such, Chamayou today poses the question of how war is even to be defined anymore. He exemplifies this with a pointed juxtaposition of kamikaze and drone pilots, which he links to the age-old metaphysical question of the mortality and immortality of body and spirit: "The kamikaze: *My body is a weapon*. The drone: *My weapon has no body*. The former implies the death of the agent. The latter totally excludes it. Kamikazes are those for whom death is certain. Drone pilots are those for whom death is impossible."[42]

What from the perspective of earlier military ethics was seen only as an extreme last resort or remained entirely outside the norm of symmetrical military combat is today the normal state or military abnormality, namely, a maximally asymmetrical contest. The military dream or "democratic" phantasm of a war without death on one side, certain death on the other. The person who deploys or guides a drone cannot be killed, but precisely by so doing causes the contingent deaths of civilians – and not simply as *collateral* damage. This radical contingency that can befall anyone at any time necessarily accompanies the massive technological dominance of one side of a given military conflict.

Then as now, from kamikaze pilots to suicide bombers, the technologically inferior must maximally capitalize on their own deaths; their goal now must be to claim as many civilian lives as possible. From a philosophical or even just dialectical perspective, then, the helplessness of one side is not so different from the superiority of the other. Behind the absolute asymmetry, we observe the contours of a diabolical symmetry and consensus that can be seen in real political terms in the mutual understanding of the hardliners and extremists in a given conflict.

Following Chamayou, we ultimately have to deal in our new century with two new ethical and metaphysical military dis/orders. "What is taking place before our very eyes is," first, "a switch from one official ethic to another: from an ethic of self-sacrifice and courage to one of self-preservation and more or less assumed cowardice," and, second, a "clash between these new weapons and the old [...] military ethos."[43] Even the makers of this new world (dis)order evidently can no longer find their bearings amidst their now contradictory basic ethical and metaphysical assumptions.

THE ABSOLUTE SUBJECT – Hannah Arendt once described the "problem of an absolute" as "the most troublesome of all problems in revolutionary government."[44] This observation is also relevant to a metaphysically informed politics of the future. For whether we want to acknowledge it or not, today we are again living in a revolutionary age in the fullest sense of the word, an age that is twisting and turning everything which came before and that stands at the beginning or origin of new political dis/orders or ab-normalities. The accompanying crisis of our society is not least an ideological crisis affecting the core of our self-understanding. Precisely in the social and political realms, the question at hand is what it means for a culture when its fundamental concepts and assumptions no longer obtain. How do we conceive political sovereignty outside of a territorial or national (and nationalistic) logic? How do we deal with the growing importance of offshore and free-trade zones that promote their own tax and labor laws and are increasingly becoming independent actors and indeed competitors of traditional nation states? What other new political subjects – reactionary terrorists as well as refugees or young climate activists seeking a different, better future – will we encounter, or which do we need given current geopolitical shifts and tensions?

For now, not only do we have no ready answers to these questions, but our politicians seem to systematically evade them. This is most clear with respect to *the* new political subject of the twenty-first century, the refugee. It shines a bad light on contemporary society when the old forces are trying with all their might to keep these – quite possibly unwittingly and unintentionally – revolutionary subjects at bay.

Speculation

The truth will set you free. But not until it's finished with you.

David Foster Wallace

METAPHYSICS AFTER ITS END – For the past several years, we have been experiencing a renewed growth of various forms of irrationalism. Political fanaticism, social obscurantism, and private esotericism are the order of the day. Religions are in the fast lane, which as always means that their very worst aspects – restrictions on free thought, mechanisms of exclusion, intolerance – are also receiving a boost. The supposed end of metaphysics under the banner of science and enlightenment has turned out to be merely skeptical disregard for metaphysics' central questions. "*The contemporary end of metaphysics is an end which, being skeptical, could only be a religious end of metaphysics*," writes Quentin Meillassoux.[1] What remained or remains unthought returns in the social psyche as a symptom, no differently than how psychoanalysis described the destiny of the individually repressed.

The return of religion is symptomatic of an intellectual failure. If philosophy does not ultimately want to content itself in the future with its self-imposed irrelevance, then it must (once again and with renewed intensity) intellectually grapple with metaphysical themes and phenomena – even if this understandably no longer comes easily to it given its history. Philosophy either trusts in its speculative force and confidently allies itself with metaphysical questions, or it will continue to be marginalized (for still being too metaphysical) by those ubiquitous specialists in matters of transcendence who bank on irrationalism. Then as tomorrow, the emergence from our self-imposed nonage described by Kant is a metaphysical affair.

THE NEW RELIGION OF DATA – The religious is returning in different ways in different fields. In the political arena, of which the secularization of theological concepts such as sovereignty and omnipotence is constitutive in the first place, we increasingly observe an instrumentalization of religious folklore in the service of conservative or reactionary politics.

In the economic realm, metaphysical thought – for Marx, not only individual commodities but also capitalism itself were "abounding in metaphysical subtleties and theological niceties"[2] – continues to operate in a different way. As Cathy O'Neil writes in her book *Weapons of Math Destruction*, purportedly objective mathematical models are, like gods, utterly "opaque, their workings invisible to all but the highest priests in their domain: mathematicians and computer scientists."[3] The impenetrability and intangibility of (often pseudo-) scientific models compulsively replicates antiquated metaphysical distinctions such as that between the pure and commanding spirit and the merely executing, determined body. Also widespread is an implicit or explicit belief in allegedly unprejudiced data free of subjective, earthly, and physical idiosyncrasies.

This techno-religious submission has gone so far that Jean-Pierre Dupuy, prophet of enlightened doomsaying, speaks of a fundamental *economystification* against which only a peculiar methodological procedure can help: "The idea that the foundations of Economy can be properly examined using the methods of theology, rather than of economics itself, may seem odd, but surely it is more honest than smuggling theology in through the back door, as economists typically do."[4] Here we are dealing with the effects of a religious faith in data that for all its worship of supposed empiricism fails to recognize its own theological blindness and is willingly taken in by self-imagined apparitions. Yuval Harari has coined the term *dataism* for this phenomenon; other names include data fetishism or data fundamentalism. Chris Anderson, the former editor-in-chief of *Wired* magazine and high priest of a secularized religion of data, gave expression to this worldview in a much-discussed article: "The new availability of huge amounts of data, along with the statistical tools to crunch these numbers, offers a whole new way of understanding the world. Correlation supersedes causation, and science can advance even without coherent models, unified theories, or really any mechanistic explanation at all."[5]

Leaving aside the fact that scientific progress would not be possible without developing hypotheses and performing experiments, nearly everything about this casual assessment is also philosophically wrong. In his belief that he has risen above every deterministic mechanics, the worshipper of data sees himself as being liberated from all earthly phenomena. Every theory or model is supposed to be made superfluous by the calculation of statistics and probabilities. Correlation (between the world and these illustrative data) rather than causation appears as the only saving option. The world is thus plugged into the wrong formula.

WHY SECULARIZATION IS NEVER ENOUGH – The medieval dictum *philosophia ancilla theologiae* – "philosophy is the handmaid of theology" – demonstrates just how close was the historical relationship between metaphysics and religion. Theo-logia as the effort to understand God and philo-sophia as love of wisdom would thus be united in their effort to ascertain the ultimate reasons of being. Jacques Derrida saw in this an ontotheology that could never be entirely deconstructed.

Modern philosophy has of course largely been a catalyst for a general secularization of culture, at once both its trigger and its result. But what if part of the problem lies precisely in this notion of "secularization"? Perhaps, as Giorgio Agamben writes, "we must distinguish between secularization and profanation. Secularization is a form of repression. It leaves intact the forces it deals with by simply moving them from one place to another. Thus, the political secularization of theological concepts (the transcendence of God as a paradigm of sovereign power) does nothing but displace the heavenly monarchy onto an earthly monarchy, leaving its power intact. Profanation, however, neutralizes what it profanes."[6] A future metaphysics will have to be a profane metaphysics, one that will root out and combat theological tendencies not only in twenty-first-century political culture, but also in other discourses and academic fields.

RETREAT WITH CONSEQUENCES – Our purportedly anti-metaphysical abstention from making absolute statements or statements about the absolute has maneuvered us down a cultural and political dead end. In the absence of any resistance, religions today are increasingly assuming the right to reclaim their supposed intellectual supremacy in sociopolitical affairs, a claim that was previously (and rightly!) believed to have been dispensed with once and for all. Parallel to this, we are experiencing an immediate and unmediatable confrontation between liberal democracies, on the one hand, and political extremists and religious fundamentalists, on the other.

Confronted by fanatics of various orientations, those disposed toward liberal democracy and schooled in deconstructive defense are often left with only moral appeals. What is lacking are more intellectual debates about how to make rational arguments even on uncertain metaphysical terrain. Not simply because "philosophy" is culturally important in and of itself and thus worth protecting, but because a new confrontation with metaphysics is once again the order of the day, first and foremost for social and political reasons. For a long time now, philosophy has gradually and shamefacedly been turning away from what was once its core competency for metaphysical questions, and society as a whole has been paying the price.

FIDEISM AND THE DE-ABSOLUTIZATION OF THOUGHT – Between positivism on the one side and the reincarnation of theological claims on the other, philosophy has lost its step and with it metaphysics come to a bad end. There are a number of historical, economic, and political reasons for the rise of various forms of irrationalism, all believing that they command certainties which are insusceptible to further argument, but philosophy itself is also partly to blame; the complicity of enlightened thought consists precisely in the naive belief that it can abandon metaphysics with impunity. What may have once been historically understandable – namely, distancing itself from the boundlessness of dogmatic metaphysics – has opened the door to a dangerous instability. After two centuries of critical anti-metaphysics, we are now, in the words of Quentin Meillassoux, confronted with the following paradox: "[T]he more thought arms itself against dogmatism, the more defenceless it becomes before fanaticism."[7]

Particularly now, we must again recall a certain aggressiveness – one that Meillassoux argues is constitutive of the project of philosophy itself – against any form of religious or fanatic "thinking," which *de facto* involves not so much thought as belief, the belief that one possesses some privileged *access to the absolute*. Only harking back to the unique speculative potential of philosophy can help against this. A different future can be conceived, not with defensive critical maneuvers, but only speculatively. And only from the future will we be able to establish an actual contemporaneity with reality, a comradeship not with the past nor merely with the present, but with the future.

INFINITE LOSSES OF REALITY – Even after the end of postmodernity, we have not returned to or arrived once and for all at reality, and the feeling of a loss of reality is widespread. But is the world, or our control of it, really lost to us? Or, as the Romantic contemporaries of nascent industrialization once wondered, *are we lost to the world*? We may well be dealing here with modern variations of the general metaphysical question first posed at the turn of the eighteenth century by Gottfried Wilhelm Leibniz: *pourquoi il y a plutôt quelque chose que rien*? According to later, more existential interpretations, this is not only the question of why there is something rather than *nothing*, but the substantially heightened question of whether there is anything other than *nothingness*. Lacanian psychoanalysis calls this the crisis of the symbolic in our society.

It might be, however, that the resulting, at times manic quest for meaning is less universal than those concerned with it think. This suspicion suggests itself in light of the fact that the Oedipal subjects threatened by the retreat of the symbolic are primarily men. We can add to this the diametrically opposite observation that in the wake of the digital revolution, we are rather dealing with an excess of significance, signs, and meaning that we have overwhelming difficulty finding any order in or reference to. We are now confronted not only with a new kind of complexity, but with a new infinity.

WHAT IF THERE IS NO BEING AT ALL? – For thousands of years now, philosophy has been so strongly shaped by the question of the substantial, of immutable and eternal being, that, given their history, it can be difficult to clearly distinguish between philosophy and ontology. "Ontology or first philosophy has constituted for centuries the fundamental historical *a priori* of Western thought," writes Giorgio Agamben, adding: "Ontology is laden with the historical destiny of the West not because an inexplicable and metahistorical power belongs to being but just the contrary, because ontology is the originary place of the historical articulation between language and world."[8] Then again, resistance to this major assumption underlying Western thought – that "being" means that which remains constant and is identical with itself – can also be traced back just as far.

The identification of the verb "to be" with its quasi-theological substantialization "being" may be only a superficial effect, however, one in which Nietzsche recognized a grammatical deception: the primacy of substantive nouns over accidental predicates. Nevertheless, we must disagree with his lovely aphorism that *we cannot be rid of God so long as we still believe in grammar.* A linguistically informed view of the structure of language actually shows us that there *is* no being at all. To begin with, the original form of any word is not a noun (as Martin Heidegger, *the* twentieth-century philosopher of being, implicitly seemed to assume), but rather a predicate. What is more, structures of meaning are never the result of individual words, but only of entire sentences or at least parts of sentences. It was in this sense that Hegel defined what according to him differentiates speculative thought – or more precisely: speculative sentences – from predicative. Speculative/dialectical sentences, according to Hegel, are distinguished by a dynamic in which the supposedly substantive subject is negated by a predicate that turns out to be the actual substance. "The content is thereby in fact no longer the predicate of the subject; rather, it is the substance, the essence, and it is the concept of what it is which is being spoken of. [...] Starting from the subject as if this were an enduring ground, [thinking] on the contrary finds that by the predicate being the substance, the subject has passed over into the predicate and has thereby become sublated."[9]

What Hegel says specifically in regard to speculative concepts can be generalized: significance lies not in nouns themselves, but in recursive sentence structures. Every concept is defined by the fact that it becomes the subject of a sentence, by its predicative structure, and the expansion of a substantive noun into a sentence is a movement of generalization. Differing relations between part and whole continually emerge in this recursive movement of the sentence toward its subject. At each step, something new is produced.

BEING AND (BECOMING AND) THOUGHT – If the noun or subject of a sentence is not the substantive condition or premise of its predicate, that is, if we cannot presume any nominal being of the verb form "is" – as the third-person indicative of "to be" – then this dislodges not only the grammatical distinction between substantial noun and accidental verb, but also that between constant being and variable becoming.

The history of philosophy has thus in a way come full circle (though without simply returning us to the beginning). Early pre-Socratic philosophers posited a strict relationship between thought and being, beginning with Parmenides, according to whom only that which is – i.e. that which remains eternally constant – can be thought. Following several thousand years of philosophical history which produced more or less every possible and refuted variation of the metaphysical notion of an identity of being and thought – "being" is itself in motion and ultimately "becoming," "being" is ultimately nothing but "semblance," etc. – a specifically modern rejection of metaphysics might now be reduced to the following formula: being and thought are mutually exclusive; thought cannot grasp being at all. Even in its anti-metaphysical variant, modern skeptical philosophy thinks in terms of a strict correlation between being and thought. Modern thought thus remains related to a form of being, even where it can only infer its existence indirectly via perception.

The best expression of this correlationism of thought and being is the modern separation of epistemological concerns from questions about reality as such. The critical division of epistemology and ontology expresses a total distinction between thought and being. We are thus dealing here with a *radicalization of correlation* and concomitant *whole alteration of being and thought*. "The unthinkable," writes Meillassoux, "can only draw us back to our inability to think otherwise, rather than to the absolute impossibility of things being wholly otherwise. It then becomes clear that this trajectory culminates in the disappearance of the pretension to *think* any absolutes, *but not in the disappearance of absolutes*."[10]

FORWARD-LOOKING THOUGHT – There are a number of reasons for the increasingly negative connotations given to the concept of speculation

over the last two centuries. In everyday understanding, speculating has probably always
implied being out of touch with reality. Critical
philosophy toiled away at speculative metaphysics, as this meant arguing from abstract and
ultimately unaccounted-for principles, rather
than proceeding empirically. And with recent
fiscal experiments and the economic crises resulting from them, "speculation" has even taken on
criminal connotations.

Against this, and against the prejudice that
speculation tends to mean turning away from
the world, proponents of speculative philosophy from Alfred North Whitehead to Isabelle
Stengers have repeatedly stressed that their field
may not exclude any topic, but rather must seek
to comprehend as much of the world as possible. A visual and forward-looking dimension
has always been inscribed in speculative thought,
going back to its etymological roots (*speculari*
= to espy, to observe). Speculation is a form of
modal thinking that, while always looking to
its contemporaneous contexts and surroundings
for inspiration, does not abide in a common
present, but sees both forward and backward in
time.

ABSTRACTION, NEGATION, SPECULATION – All
thought begins with an abstraction from the
intuitively accessible world and for this reason
alone has a metaphysical component, regardless
of whether we are talking about classification,
typologization, or some other form of abstraction. For Hegel – *the* classic speculative/dialectical
philosopher – no less than for his successors and
commentators like Alexandre Kojève, abstraction
necessarily leads to negation. Thought recognizes
that things are what they are only in distinction
to other things. Day is only the opposite of night.
A letter or sound only makes sense insofar as it is
distinct from another.

Speculation takes this abstraction even further,
now negating the negation, though not in the ide-
alist sense of a synthetic sublation of difference.
Speculating always also means first (re)producing
our relationship to the world in general (what
Badiou calls "truth-processes"). The new emerges
not with reflexive recourse to what already exists
or has already been thought, but only through
further alienation. Future metaphysical speculation teaches us that we must put an end to our
fear of the alien and irreducible, including in the
realm of thought, of *noesis*. What can be called

poetic or poietic speculation – in the sense of *poiesis*, the creation of the new – aims at the mind not coming to itself, but always becoming something else, always in a process of alienation from itself. Speculative thought aims at a different future as well as an othering or alter-egoization of the ego. Ceaseless transformation of world and self. *Xenoesis*.

Notes

Introduction: Metaphysics

1 Ulrich Beck, *Risk Society: Towards a New Modernity*, trans. Mark Ritter (London: SAGE Publications, 1992), 142.

2 Martin Heidegger, *The Fundamental Concepts of Metaphysics: World, Finitude, Solitude*, trans. William McNeill and Nicholas Walker (Bloomington: Indiana University Press, 1995), 9.

3 Martin Heidegger, *Introduction to Metaphysics*, 2nd edn, trans. Gregory Fried and Richard Polt (New Haven: Yale University Press, 2014), 93.

4 Jean-Pierre Dupuy, *The Mark of the Sacred*, trans. M. B. Debevoise (Stanford: Stanford University Press, 2013), 67.

5 Frank Ruda and Agon Hamza, "An Interview with Catherine Malabou: Toward Epigenetic Philosophy," in *Crisis and Critique* 5.1 (2018), 434–447.

6 Bruno Latour, *Facing Gaia: Eight Lectures on the New Climatic Regime* (Cambridge: Polity, 2017), 90f.

7 Ludwig Wittgenstein, *Tractatus Logico-Philosophicus*, trans. D. F. Pears and B. F. McGuinness (London: Routledge, 2001), 84.

8 Wolfram Eilenberger, *Zeit der Zauberer: Das große Jahrzehnt der Philosophie 1919 – 1929* (Stuttgart: Klett-Cotta, 2018).

9 Dietmar Dath, "Ein tiefes Loch in der Natur," in *Frankfurter Allgemeine Zeitung*, March 10, 2018.

10 Rupert Sheldrake, *The Science Delusion* (London: Coronet, 2012), 18.

11 Alfred North Whitehead, *Dialogues of Alfred North Whitehead* (Boston: David R. Godine, 2001), 363.

12 Walter Benjamin, *The Origin of German Tragic Drama*, trans. John Osborne (London: Verso, 1998), 39.

13 Yuk Hui, "Algorithmic Catastrophe – The Revenge of Contingency," in *Parrhesia* 23 (2015), 122–143 (139).

14 Ibid., 122.

15 Luciana Parisi, *Contagious Architecture: Computation, Aesthetics, and Space* (Cambridge, Mass.: The MIT Press, 2013), 19.

16 Dupuy, *The Mark of the Sacred*, 27f.

17 Latour, *Facing Gaia*, 294.

18 Quentin Meillassoux, "Potentiality and Virtuality," trans. Robin Mackay, in Levi Bryant, Nick Srnicek, and Graham Harman, eds., *The Speculative Turn: Continental Materialism and Realism* (Melbourne: re.press, 2011), 224–236 (232).

19 Ibid., 231.

20 Jussi Parikka and Tony D. Sampson, eds., *The Spam*

Book: On Viruses, Porn, and Other Anomalies from the Dark Side of Digital Culture (New York: Hampton Press, 2009), 13.

21 Franco Berardi, "'How do we explain depression to ourselves?'" Bifo remembers Mark Fisher, in *Novara Media*, February 4, 2017, https://novaramedia.com/2017/02/04/how-do-we-explain-depression-to-ourselves-bifo-remembers-mark-fisher/.

22 Larry Rosen, *iDisorder: Understanding Our Obsession with Technology and Overcoming Its Hold on Us* (New York: St. Martin's Press, 2013).

23 Catherine Malabou, *The New Wounded: From Neurosis to Brain Damage*, trans. Steven Miller (New York: Fordham University Press, 2012), xiv.

24 Ibid., 5.

25 Ed Finn, *What Algorithms Want: Imagination in the Age of Computing* (Cambridge, Mass.: The MIT Press, 2017), 47.

26 Michel Foucault, *The Order of Things: An Archaeology of the Human Sciences* (New York: Vintage Books, 1994), 127f.

27 Gregory Chaitin, "Life as Evolving Software," in Hector Zenil, ed., *A Computable Universe: Understanding and Exploring Nature as Computation* (Hackensack: World Scientific Publishing Co., 2012), 297–322.

28 Immanuel Kant, *Kant on Swedenborg:* Dreams of a Spirit-Seer *and Other Writings*, ed. Gregory R. Johnson, trans. Gregory R. Johnson and Glenn Alexander Magee (West Chester: Swedenborg Foundation Publishers, 2002), 39.

29 Ibid., 39f.

30 Elizabeth A. Povinelli, *Geontologies: A Requiem to Late Liberalism* (Durham: Duke University Press, 2016), 14.

31 Michael Wheeler, "Thinking Beyond the Brain: Educating and Building, from the Standpoint of Extended Cognition," in Matteo Pasquinelli, ed., *Alleys of Your Mind: Augmented Intelligence and Its Traumas* (Lüneberg: Meson Press, 2015), 85–104 (103).

32 Benjamin H. Bratton, *The Stack: On Software and Sovereignty* (Cambridge, Mass.: The MIT Press, 2015), 364.

33 Benjamin H. Bratton, "Outing Artificial Intelligence: Reckoning with Turing Tests," in Pasquinelli, ed., *Alleys of Your Mind*, 69–80 (74).

34 Dirk Baecker, "Verstehen wir das, worüber wir reden?", in *Neue Zürcher Zeitung*, March 2, 2018.

35 Stephen Buranyi, "Rise of the racist robots – how AI is learning all our worst impulses," *Guardian*, August 8, 2017, https://www.theguardian.com/inequality/2017/aug/08/rise-of-the-racist-robots-how-ai-is-learning-all-our-worst-impulses.

36 Benjamin H. Bratton, "The City Wears Us: Notes on the Scope of Distributed Sensing and Sensation," in *Glass Bead* 1: *Site 1: Logic Gate, the Politics of the Artifactual Mind* (2017), http://www.glass-bead.org/article/city-wears-us-notes-scope-distributed-sensing-sensation/?lang=enview.

Changing Times

1 Rob Nixon, *Slow Violence and the Environmentalism of the Poor* (Cambridge, Mass.: Harvard University Press, 2011), 2.

2 Daniel Falb, *Geospekulationen: Metaphysik für die Erde im Anthropozän* (Berlin: Merve, 2019).

3 Sebastian Rödl, *Categories of the Temporal*, trans. Sibylle Salewski (Cambridge, Mass.: Harvard University Press, 2012), 42f.

4 Ibid., 57.

5 Ibid., 79.

6 Latour, *Facing Gaia*, 242f.

7 Michio Kaku, *Physics of the Future: How Science Will Shape Human Destiny and Our Daily Lives by the Year 2100* (New York: Anchor, 2012), 114.

8 Finn, *What Algorithms Want*, 160.

9 Ibid., 50.

10 Arjun Appadurai, *Banking on Words: The Failure of Language in the Age of Derivative Finance* (Chicago: University of Chicago Press, 2016), 152.

11 Grégoire Chamayou, *A Theory of the Drone*, trans. Janet Lloyd (New York: The New Press, 2015), 32.

12 Ibid., 68.

13 Parisi, *Contagious Architecture*, xiii.

14 Ibid., 71.

15 Terrence W. Deacon, *Incomplete Nature: How Mind Emerged from Matter* (New York: W. W. Norton, 2012), 36f.

16 Kaku, *Physics of the Future*, 82.

17 R. Scott Bakker, "The Last Magic Show: A Blind

Brain Theory of the Appearance of Consciousness," 2. Available at https://www.academia.edu/1502945/The_Last_Magic_Show_A_Blind_Brain_Theory_of_the_Appearance_of_Consciousness.

18 James Trafford, "Re-engineering Commonsense," in *Glass Bead* 1 (2017), http://www.glass-bead.org/article/re-engineering-commonsense/?lang=enview.

19 James Lovelock, *A Rough Ride to the Future* (London: Allen Lane, 2014), 64.

20 Donna Haraway, *Staying with the Trouble: Making Kin in the Chthulucene* (Durham: Duke University Press, 2016), 33.

21 Gary Tomlinson, "Semiotic Epicycles and Emergent Thresholds in Human Evolution," in *Glass Bead* 1 (2017).

22 Bakker, *The Last Magic Show*.

23 Terrence W. Deacon, *The Symbolic Species: The Co-evolution of Language and the Brain* (New York: W. W. Norton, 1997), 122.

24 Walter Benjamin, "On Language as Such and on the Language of Man," in *Selected Writings*, vol. 1: *1913–1926*, eds. Marcus Bullock and Michael W. Jennings (Cambridge, Mass.: Harvard University Press, 1996), 62–74 (63).

25 Finn, *What Algorithms Want*, 5.

26 Tomlinson, "Semiotic Epicycles."

27 Finn, *What Algorithms Want*, 62.

28 Charles Sanders Peirce, *Collected Papers of Charles Sanders Peirce*, vol. 5: *Pragmatism and Pragmaticism* (Cambridge, Mass.: Harvard University Press, 1935), 106.

29 Steven Shaviro, *Discognition* (London: Repeater, 2016), 12.

30 Ray Brassier, "Concepts and Objects," in Bryant et al., eds., *The Speculative Turn*, 47, 49.

31 Bruno Latour, *Pandora's Hope: Essays on the Reality of Science Studies* (Cambridge, Mass.: Harvard University Press, 1999), 69.

32 Quentin Meillassoux, "Metaphysics, Speculation, Correlation," in *Pli: The Warwick Journal of Philosophy* 22 (2011), 3–25 (12).

33 M. Rainer Lepsius, *Institutionalisierung politischen Handelns: Analysen zur DDR, Wiedervereinigung und Europäischen Union* (Wiesbaden: Springer VS, 2013), 14.

34 Jacques Rancière, *Dis-agreement: Politics and Philosophy*, trans. Julie Rose (Minneapolis: University of Minnesota Press, 1999), 28.

35 Ibid., 30.

36 Davor Vidas, "When the Sea Beings to Dominate the Land," in *Technosphere Magazine*, April 15, 2017, https://technosphere-magazine.hkw.de/p/When-the-Sea-Begins-to-Dominate-the-Land-xcY33UY61frB2X4JTntqhD. Cf. Davor Vidas, "The Anthropocene and the International Law of the Sea," in *Philosophical Transactions of the Royal Society A: Mathematical, Physical and Engineering Sciences* 369/1938 (2011), 914.

37 Ibid.

38 Chamayou, 57.

39 Ibid., 54.

40 Ibid., 64.

41 Ibid., 16f.

42 Ibid., 84.

43 Ibid., 101, 99.

44 Hannah Arendt, *On Revolution* (New York: Penguin, 2006), 149.

Speculation

1 Quentin Meillassoux, *After Finitude: An Essay on the Necessity of Contingency*, trans. Ray Brassier (London: Continuum, 2008), 46.

2 Karl Marx, *Capital: A Critique of Political Economy*, vol. 1, trans. Ben Fowkes (London: Penguin, 1990), 163.

3 Cathy O'Neil, *Weapons of Math Destruction: How Big Data Increases Inequality and Threatens Democracy* (New York: Crown, 2016), 3.

4 Jean-Pierre Dupuy, *Economy and the Future: A Crisis of Faith*, trans. M. B. DeBevoise (East Lansing: Michigan State University Press, 2014), 56.

5 Chris Anderson, "The End of Theory: The Data Deluge Makes the Scientific Method Obsolete," in *Wired*, June 23, 2008.

6 Giorgio Agamben, *Profanations*, trans. Jeff Fort (New York: Zone Books, 2007), 77.

7 Meillassoux, *After Finitude*, 48.

8 Giorgio Agamben, *The Use of Bodies (Homo Sacer IV, 2)*, trans. Adam Kotsko (Stanford: Stanford University Press, 2016), 112, 111.

9 Georg Wilhelm Friedrich Hegel, *The Phenomenology of Spirit*, trans. Terry Pinkard (Cambridge: Cambridge University Press, 2018), 38.

10 Meillassoux, *After Finitude*, 44.

Index